DRIPPING WITH FAVOR
Breaking Mindsets that hinder Destiny

By Danny Casas Jr.

Endorsements

Favored people are often catalysts God uses to fuel and facilitate His work. God's favor upon Danny's life is apparent to all who know and love him, so it's easy to see why God has called him to write this book. From my perspective, the most favored people walk with grace and gentleness, not swagger. They exhibit Christian graces in even the most difficult of circumstances. Pastor Danny is this type of man. I pray this book touches lives beyond the limits of what can even be imagined. May God bless the reader with the favor of God.

Tom Watson, *Senior Pastor, Aspire Church, Manchester, England*

Dripping With Favor is definitely a must read! When we consider our 10 years of Jesus Ministry, we can say this past year has been nothing but the best! In this book, you will experience the story of a group of people, who through every adversity, overcome and continue to strive to experience and bring God's kingdom here on earth. Do not sleep on this!

Andrea & Eric Gonzales, *Creative Leaders, Remnant Church, Whittier, California*

In his first book, Through the Eyes of a Prodigal, Pastor Danny Casas Jr. draws parallels between the story of the prodigal son and his own life and upbringing. It is a relevant story of hope and redeeming love. In his new book, Dripping with Favor, he draws you into this book by providing Biblical understanding and principles that are presented in a practical and accessible way that is easy to follow. His repertoire for delivering the Gospel to the old and new generation is evident in his ministries today, which draws on experience, Biblical education, and applying those Biblical principles.

Ignacio Torres, *Senior Pastor, Legacy Church, Salinas, California*

Unforgiveness certainly can become a great blockade to God's blessings in our lives. This book certainly provides powerful key principles on how to live your life with the favor God has placed upon you. It will help you learn how to forgive so that you are brought out of confinement, and into alignment to be released to your assignment in the kingdom of God.

Edwin Melendez, *Senior Pastor, Culture City Church, Chicago, Illinois*

"The man is the message; the message is the man" is a quote that is very dear to me. Pastor Danny's book exemplifies this quote. The messages that fill this book come from a man who has lived out principles from the Word of God authenticating the inerrancy of the scriptures, "you reap what you sow." The vessel is as important as the message that he promotes because he is and lives the message. Pastor Danny is a vessel filled with grace and truth, which is evident as it flows through the pages of this book. He is a messenger living a life "dripping with favor." Learn from the vessel.

George Cresencia, *Pastor, Missionary, Evangelist, Remnant Church, Whittier, California*

Contents

Dedication

Foreword

Acknowledgments

Introduction

Chapter One: Favor in unlikely places.........................17

Chapter Two: Dreams of the Favored.........................26

Chapter Three: A Favored Mindset.............................39

Chapter Four: Favored to Forgive 49

Chapter Five: Favored to Fast....................................59

Chapter Six: God favors the Humble 70

Chapter Seven: Favored with Provision 87

Chapter Eight: United by Favor.................................104

Chapter Nine: Resting in His Favor 117

Chapter Ten: Favored by Thanksgiving......................127

Chapter Eleven: Favored for Success........................137

Dedication

To the volunteers and members of Remnant Church of Whittier, your dedication to Christ and labor of love is transforming the world. We are so grateful to partner with you all as we honor our Lord and Savior Jesus Christ.

Foreword

It was Sunday, January 27, 2013, when my family and I took a trip to the city of Porterville. A small rural city located in the outskirts of Central California. I was invited by a good friend to preach at his church. At the time, Pastor Danny Casas Jr. was the Pastor of his first church plant, New Harvest Porterville. Growing up in church, I was always around a fellowship of churches and made friends over the years with brothers and sisters from all over the country who went on to do amazing works for God.

One of my long-lasting memories of the trip to Porterville was seeing firsthand, the heart of humility, displayed by Pastor Danny and his wife, Sabrina. We had a great time at the Sunday service, and we got to spend time with them after enjoying good food and fellowship. We caught up on the great things God was doing in Porterville and in our fellowship of churches. Anytime brothers and sisters in Christ come together, you always walk away encouraged, refreshed and reminded of one thing, "We are all in this together." I had seen Pastor Danny grow up in the church as a teenager and as a young preacher who was on fire for God. His father, Pastor Danny Casas Sr., is the pastor and founder of an amazing church in the city of Fresno. I recognized Pastor Danny as a "PK" (a pastor´s kid).

As the years went on, I saw Pastor Danny at youth

conferences and church events. Seeing Pastor Danny answer the call and become a pastor, I recalled being deeply inspired by his life and was blessed to build a friendship with him and his family over the years. I vividly remember talking to Pastor Danny and seeing his joy and excitement about the things God was doing in his church. On the drive home from Porterville, I remember thinking, "God's favor is upon Pastor Danny and his beautiful family."

During that season, I was honored to be leading a Young Adults ministry in the City of Azusa. It was a special time. Collaboration with other churches was so important as we contended for a move of God in our generation. We were hungry, and we were desperately wanting God to set us on fire so we could impact others and reach our cities for Jesus.

Fast forward to the year 2020. The year of the pandemic. Once again, we were brought together by a God ordained move, and I now find myself co-laboring side by side with Pastor Danny in church ministry. The year 2020 was many things for many people. Chaos. Tragedy. Pain. Change. Healing. But through God's sovereign path, He carried my family and I into a new environment, amongst a new group of brothers and sisters in Christ. Now as we pressed through the difficult year, I witnessed firsthand, God's favor and protection upon Pastor Danny, his family and our dear friends and pastors who decided to take a stand for righteousness.

I continued my partnership with Pastor Danny and saw firsthand that through change, obstacles, pain and opposition, God's favor was upon a group of brothers and sisters in Christ who wanted to do something new for the Kingdom of God. From the onset, I was excited to be working with Pastor Danny and other great pastors and leaders who shared the same heart, the same passion and the same goal. That goal was to be humble before God, maintain a clean heart and believe for God's favor as we endeavored in this new journey, a church plant, in the city of Whitter.

Coming off his first book, Through the Eyes of a Prodigal, Pastor Danny continues his journey as a writer with his second book, Dripping with Favor. Sharing firsthand accounts and experiences of seeking and experiencing God's favor, Pastor Danny provides us with powerful life lessons that can be applied to our everyday life as a believer in Christ.

But what is favor? Is favor sometimes confused with obtaining success, wealth and possession? Or is God's favor something much more? A seasoned Christian would agree, to obtain God's favor, one must go through a series of highs and lows in their spiritual walk and place their trust in Jesus believing that He will see you through every step of the way. That journey can result in a series of opportunities for us to give the circumstance, trial or situation to God and trust that His hand of favor and protection is with us.

From letting go of past pain and moving forward, to letting God use your story to reach others for Jesus, Pastor Danny shares practical steps to seek God's favor for your life. Pastor Danny uses scripture, his pastoral experience and his journey as a believer in Christ to bring us into a deeper understanding of what it means to be "Dripping with Favor."

I pray you are encouraged, refreshed and positioned towards seeking God's favor for your own life.

George Zendejas, *Vision Leader, Remnant Church of Whittier, California*

Acknowledgements

To my beautiful wife Sabrina, thank you for believing in me, praying for me, and encouraging me to honor Christ at all cost. You have been a constant encouragement in my life. I love you with all my heart.

A special thanks to my parents Pastor Danny and Barbara Casas and the Remnant church of Fresno for providing biblical direction, encouragement and financial support when we needed it most.

Thank you to my friends Joseph and Angie Pasos. Your friendship has been a constant blessing throughout the years.

A special thank you to S.H.I.F.T. Ministries, for your leadership and example of integrity, truly "Together, we can!"

I also want to thank Pastor Ignacio and Sara Torres of Legacy church of Salinas. Thank you for your continued mentorship for many years.

A sincere thanks to Pastor Tim and Maryann Echevarria, your encouragement, support and genuine love will never be forgotten.

To Pastor Phil and Pat Aguilar of San Diego City Church, thank you for your leadership and faithful daily reminders for morning prayer.

A special thank you to Pastor George Cresencia for your continued well of supernatural insights and revelation.

A special thanks to Jim Jimenez Jr. for his amazing creativity in designing the book cover. Also, his love for Christ he exhales to all who come near him.

To Brother Felix and Sister Estrella and Dennis De Ocampo, thank you for your continuous prayers and love.

I want to thank Pastor Dan Pryor and the Plymouth church of Whittier for graciously allowing us to use their patio area when we didn't have a home. May the Lord continue to richly bless you.

Thank you to Gabe and Angel Pulido, your prayers from years ago are still felt today.

A special thank you to Pastor Herbert Percy and the Trinity Lutheran congregation for your partnership with Remnant church of Whittier, truly we are together in Christ.

To the Team Leaders and volunteers of Remnant Church of Whittier, my wife and I extend our deepest gratitude. Your love for God is evident by the way you love others.

All proceeds from this book will be donated to the Remnant Church of Whittier's Building fund. It will be a place of Spirit filled worship, vibrant ministry, apologetics, Christian Education, and community.

Introduction

When Christ came to earth, everything changed forever. His life, death and resurrection broke carnal paradigms that had plagued mankind for eons. One of the aspects of Christs' mission was to release captives from chains that held them shackled for far too long (Isaiah 61:1). When Christ accomplished His mission to save mankind, every curse had to bow down at the name of Jesus. Joy, peace, self-control, righteousness, and FAVOR are fruits of Christs' precious and priceless sacrifice.

Sadly, some Christians are living like heaven isn't real, and that the name of Jesus doesn't possess any power. These misguided mindsets leave us stuck in negative paradigms of thinking. These mindsets are counterintuitive, harmful and hopeless. In each chapter we will cover these misguided mindsets and expose them.

Conversely, we will also be looking at the favored mindset. As we look into the life of Joseph from the book of Genesis, we'll see this young man was dripping with favor from a very young age. Nevertheless, he faced trial after trial, and yet he witnessed firsthand the Sovereignty of God at work in his life. The applications from his life will connect the dots in ours. We may find ourselves surprised--we have a lot in common with Joseph. His perseverance and trust in God will refresh you to continue forward.

Favor is powerful and affects our thoughts and actions on so many different levels. Favor is the game-changer that takes a person from having a misguided mindset to having the mind of Christ. As you read through the pages of this book, you'll discover portions titled, "the Favored Mindset," to encourage you in your walk with God. You will discover the purpose and place for favor in each and every believer's life. In every chapter, as we look at the Favored Mindset, we'll find out what that means, looks like, and requires of us as faithful believers. I purposely tailored every chapter to include this Favored Mindset in the hopes it will provide a new way of seeing yourself through the light of Scripture. I believe this book could change your life forever. If you read these words by faith and allow the verses to penetrate your heart, you will never be the same. You'll be dripping in God's Favor.

Are you ready?
Let's do this!

Favor in Unlikely Places

"But while Joseph was there in the prison, the LORD was with him; he showed him kindness and granted him favor in the eyes of the prison warden"

- Genesis 39:20-21

"There is no attribute of God more comforting to His children than the doctrine of Divine Sovereignty. Under the most adverse circumstances, in the most severe troubles, they believe that Sovereignty hath ordained their afflictions, that Sovereignty overrules them, and that Sovereignty will sanctify them all."

- Charles Spurgeon[1]

The Remnant Church of Whittier started on September 23, 2020, at Hermosillo Park in the county of Los Angeles. That beautiful Wednesday evening will forever be etched on the hearts of parishioners of Remnant.

---

[1] https://www.azquotes.com/quote/565227, accessed August 8, 2021.

What made it unique was that it took place in a park. Of all places, God chose to birth a church in a park. Every church has a story, and every church is unique. Our story is a faith-filled, crazy, favor-dripping story; full of miracles and wonders from day one.

From a natural perspective, the situation looked unfavorable. We were up against so many odds. Below are a few:

- *We had no money--not a dime, literally.*
- *We had no fancy media equipment.*
- *We had no sound equipment.*
- *We had no chairs.*
- *We had no restrooms.*
- *And we were in the middle of a global pandemic.*

If you have ever heard anyone say, "To start a church, you need to be a little crazy," then you've heard the truth.

We didn't even have a set plan of what to do. From day one, it was evident that God was involved in the "Planning Stages" as well as the execution of this. Modern day church planting committees would have scoffed at Remnant doing what we knew God was calling us to do. No disrespect to the experts, but when God calls you to plant a church, you don't need a seven-phase plan to proceed forward. You just need to know that you know ~~that~~ He is able, and if He is able, you'll be fine.

Any logical church consulting firm would have encouraged us to schedule a one-year church planting plan and gradually proceed and conduct an in-depth study of the target demographics. There were a lot of things we didn't have, but we had what mattered most, the Most-High, He was in our midst, and we were dripping with His favor.

- *We didn't have money, but we were overflowing with a spirit of generosity.*

- *We didn't have a facility, but we had a genuine spirit of community.*

- *We didn't have a fancy sound system, but we had a heart to worship.*

- *We had nothing, but like Paul writes in 2 Corinthians 6:10, "sorrowful, yet always rejoicing; poor, yet making many rich; having nothing, and yet possessing everything."*

As I drove to the park that first evening, I wondered if anyone would show up. All we had was the word of mouth and a social media post that we were going to meet for prayer at the park. The closer I got to the park, with the beautiful Los Angeles sunlight slowly drifting towards the Pacific Ocean, I became more confident that God was involved--His Presence was present. That's all I needed.

I stepped foot out of my car to walk to the impromptu prayer meeting at the park, and I walked towards the oval outdoor amphitheater. As I came closer, I sensed the Presence of the Lord in a powerful way. It was a glorious evening full of vibrant worship to God and heartfelt prayer for the Lord's direction and strength. None of us knew exactly what was taking place, but our eyes were looking to heaven. In a way I hadn't experienced before, I sensed His glorious Presence, but it wasn't only me, many of us there that night cried, worshipped, and cried some more. The Glory of God flooded the park that evening. Evident by supernatural joy, prophecy, freedom, and an overwhelming sense of God's perfect Peace. As we raised our hands in worship and lifted our voices in praise to our King, He invaded the park. This was truly favor in an unlikely place.

Looking back, we were all in a delivery room that evening, and a new church plant was getting ready to be born. A church whose hearts' desire was to find God's heart. A church that is mission-field minded, never getting cozy in our four walls, but constantly on the offensive to win the young and old with the greatest story ever told: The Gospel Story.

The decision to start the church that fateful evening didn't rest on man's wisdom or strength, but it rested directly upon the Sovereignty of God and the Commission of Christ to go forth and make disciples (Matthew 28:19). It was no coincidence of what took place, where it took place, and with whom it took place. God doesn't make mistakes. He is a God of order, creativity, structure, and purpose. The Bible says, "For the LORD Almighty has purposed, and who can thwart him? His hand is stretched out, and who can turn it back?" (Isaiah 14:27). Even before the foundations of the world were laid, God saw us at the park and sees what the future holds. Relating that to your life, God sees your beginning, your current state, and your future, and in all of these, He has placed His favor over your life to help you just as Paul writes to the church in Ephesus "to walk in good works" (Ephesians 2:10).

Misguided Mindset:
God Placed Me in the Wrong Place

Have you ever been in a place where you felt like the favor of God has departed from your life? Perhaps a job lost, a broken dream, or a destiny that seemed destroyed? What do you do in times like this? Times when discouragement seems to be living in your head like a migraine headache that won't go away. When the clear charted course becomes nebulous because of hurt, rejection, and heartbreak. All these can cause the fog of confusion to set in. During these circumstances, we may ask ourselves, "where is God," and, "am I in the wrong place?" Where is the favor that He promises in His Word during these times?

We have all experienced these moments that can lead us to doubt that God's favor is resting upon our lives. As we look all throughout the Word of God, we witness stories of people who faced extreme opposition but who were dripping with God's favor, even in bleak places. From Genesis to Revelations we get a front row seat of women and men of God who fought by faith and seen the favor of God in hard places.

For example, let's look at the life of Joseph, a man who God had destined for greatness. He dreamed great dreams as a young man, and he was highly favored by his father. Yet, God in His Providence allowed setbacks and injustice to make him the man that would become, second-in-command over all of Egypt.

- *God allowed him to be sold as a slave.*
- *God allowed him to be falsely accused and convicted.*
- *God even allowed him to go to prison.*

In all these unfavorable places and circumstances, we find a promise in God's Word that will keep us in each and every situation. Only in allowing God's Word to transform our minds can we break free from the misguided mindset of thinking "God placed me in the wrong place."

Sadly, some believers don't recognize how God puts us in unfavorable places to prepare us for our future. We all can find ourselves just focusing on how we got the short end of the stick, on what we lost, and how others misused and abused us. Yes, we are to acknowledge our journey, but we are also to enjoy the journey. And that means forgiving others, looking ahead with expectation, and not having a victim mentality. We are not victims, we are victors (1 Corinthians 15:57). This is the mindset we need to possess and remember-- God doesn't make mistakes and He never places me in the wrong place.

Favored Mindset:
God Never Places Me in the Wrong Place

> *"But while Joseph was there in the prison, the LORD was with him; he showed him kindness and granted him favor in the eyes of the prison warden"*
>
> *- Genesis 39:20-21*

In the Sovereignty of God, Joseph was placed as Jacob's son. Then Joseph was placed in Potiphar's house. Then Joseph was placed in prison. And finally, Joseph was placed as the prince of all of Egypt. In each and every season of Joseph's life, he was in the right place because God had sent him there. Each place was a steppingstone to the next assignment. All the places tied into each other.

The same is true for us. In every moment of our lives, there is no mistake where God sends us. In His omnipotence He places us in each season for a reason and in each place with a purpose. He is prepping us, molding us, and shaping us into the image of His Son. There are no mistakes. Nothing gets passed God's table without His full attention. He doesn't place us in an area that isn't part of His perfect plan. Many times, when we face opposition, we are tempted to believe we are in the wrong place. When opposition could be a sign that we are in the right place of God's perfect and pleasing will. It's in opposition that we learn to trust God, to seek Him and to be obedient to His Word.

Even looking at all the miracles that God has done for our church. Our starting point was a park, then a parking lot, then a patio, and finally a gym. Each and every place God's favor rested upon us. And wherever God places us next, it will be the place that He ordained for us before the creation of the universe. There aren't any mistakes with where you're at when you're walking in obedience to Christ. Of course, sometimes that's hard to believe, but we can trust Him that made that promise. The Remnant Church of Whittier trusted God and that His promises are true for today and also for the future. God gets all the glory. It has been Him every step of the way. He is writing our story, and we love the first chapter--how from a humble prayer meeting of hungry believers, a church emerged. A dream came true.

Prayer of Favor

Lord, thank You for being with me in every place that You have sent me. I trust fully in Your promise that You will never leave me or forsake me. Even when times are hard and I want to run away from the place that You have put me, I will stay by faith. I know that You are molding me into the person that You want me to become. I will wait on You for your continued strength and courage in my journey in this life. You have a destiny for my life and no matter where You have placed me, Your favor is dripping over my life. Thank You Lord. All this I ask in the mighty Name of Jesus, Amen.

Dreams of the Favored

"So Joseph went after his brothers and found them near Dothan. But they saw him in the distance, and before he reached them, they plotted to kill him. "Here comes that dreamer!" they said to each other. "Come now, let's kill him and throw him into one of these cisterns and say that a ferocious animal devoured him. Then we'll see what comes of his dreams."

- Genesis 37:17-20

"You are never too old to set another goal or to dream a new dream."

– C.S. Lewis[2]

When we were kids, we had great dreams. The aspirations of our childhood and teenage years can be the catalyst for an amazing future. We have all witnessed friends and family who have persevered on the long road and have seen their God-given dreams come to

[2] https://www.positivityblog.com/quotes-on-dreams/, accessed August 8, 2021.

fruition. Seeing them accomplish and celebrate those dreams reminds us that it's all worth it. Whether they are dancing down the aisle at their graduation, wedding, or retirement, we celebrate with them!

The key word that got them to their finish-line of fulfillment is "persevered." Surely there were seasons when they wanted to quit, but they didn't. They faced meager beginnings, piles of homework, and mean people, nevertheless, they persevered. Many of them faced job demotions, job terminations, and financial hardships, yet they persevered. Others encountered being lied about, being ostracized, and having their character assassinated, however they persevered. As a result of their perseverance, they are blessed!

My wife and I are so grateful to be the pastors of Remnant Church here in the beautiful city of Whittier, California. Truly, a dream come true, and this church is most definitely a miracle. Our community of believers has a heart to know God. We have been through some great times and some rough times, but through it all God has showered us with His favor. Only the hand of Christ could have sovereignly orchestrated what is taking place in our church. I want to share the story of our church, and from this amazing story transpose certain truths of how Christ bestows His favor, and how to recognize His favor in our lives and in the lives of others.

There have been many obstacles that we faced in our first year as a church, but we continued to persevere. Every God-given dream that we have possessed has been faced with resistance, but we have continued to believe that God is going to provide strength, and He always does. For example, our building situation has been challenging, but we know that someday we are going to own our own facility, with a worship center, school of ministry, prayer hall, and missions center. All the proceeds from this very book you hold are going to be invested towards that reality.

In Scripture, the book of Genesis records the astounding story of Joseph. This young man received God-given dreams about his future. These dreams predicted favor, promotion, wisdom, and leadership in his life. Instead of humbly keeping these dreams to himself and watching God unfold them, he impatiently touted the dreams to his brothers and father. As many of us know, this was not a wise decision. Sometimes it's best to remain silent and be confident in God's promises knowing He will work through us instead of broadcasting these promises to others. Sometimes there will be people who aren't as much about the dreams that God gives us. Then some people are like Joseph's brothers who sadly were ready to kill him! They hated his dreams, and they despised the apparent favor that was dripping in his life. Although they tried to destroy the dreamer, God used the apparent misfortune to accomplish His divine plan. One verse that can puzzle all this together is when Paul writes in Romans 8:28, "And we know that all things God works together for the good to those who love him, who have been called according to his purpose." Joseph loved God and all the bad things that took place set him on the right trajectory towards his dreams becoming a reality. If these bad things didn't transpire, the greater good would not have been accomplished. For example, let's say 17-year-old Joseph told his brothers and father about the dreams God had given him, and instead of hating on him they celebrated him. What if they shielded him and served him in their Middle Eastern house? Giving him the biggest room, best clothes, and never letting him lift a finger. What if they never let him experience harm or insult? Consequently, always over protecting their favored, little brother.

In God's providence the famine would have still came, but they wouldn't have sent Joseph to Egypt to help them secure the needed food for them and their families to survive. As a result, in this scenario, they all would have died. Their sheltering of Joseph would have led to countless deaths due to starvation because there wouldn't have been storehouses of food available. Sovereignly, God sent Joseph ahead of his family to prepare the way, to save the food, to administer a plan that would unfold the dream in a fashion that only God could orchestrate. Difficult things could make us bitter, or they can make us stronger, wiser, and more compassionate. I like choosing the latter.

An example of this is when we exercise. The benefits are numerous when we lift weights, go swimming, walking, or jogging. From these exercise activities, we grow stronger through resistance. Without resistance our muscles will atrophy. It's through resistance that we grow stronger!

For all of us there is a process that is required of us. If we dream to become a great musician, jiu-jitsu competitor, or established writer, it is going to take practice and process. Practice has to do with consistent repetition, while process has to do with dry times and moving forward during seasons where you lack fulfillment. For example, in anything we set out to accomplish there is going to be times when we want to quit because of the lack of results or progress. If the process is lacking progress, you'll be experiencing the following:

Waiting. There will be times when we want to quit on our dreams. As aforementioned, we all have a "process" of preparation to embark on. Waiting isn't fun. Whether it's for that spouse who loves God, or that job that doesn't remove you from faith-filled community, we can all agree that it's some hard work to wait on God. There is no "fast pass" to seeing our dreams fulfilled. It's a long road, but it's worth the wait.

Sabotage. On the journey there is going to be some things that take place that can clearly look like sabotage. There can be instances when it seems like things that shouldn't happen are taking place. The dreams that God has given us can look like they have been destroyed by the mistakes of others. Case in point: Joseph's brothers unlawfully sold him as a slave (Genesis 37:27). This disgraceful act seems to sabotage the dreams that Joseph had, but it set him on a trajectory for his dreams to become a reality. This apparent act of sabotage was actually an act of God.

Rejection. Just like Joseph was rejected by his brothers, we too will experience rejection from others. We have all been in that place when others we loved or looked up to, distanced themselves from us. We can feel abandoned, alone, and rejected. In those seasons of rejection, we can become disorientated and disenchanted with life and ministry. In these moments the enemy works overtime leading us to subscribe to a mindset that will lead us to abandon our dreams.

Misguided Mindset:
My Dreams Will Never Come into Fruition

There is a graveyard full of dreams that were once alive and vibrant. Dreams that were meant to change the world, travel the world, and inspire the world. Dreams that lived, believed, and dwelt in the hearts of God's people. Dreams that lived in the young and the old. God-breathed dreams creatively fabricated in the heart of the Dream Giver, God Himself.

Sadly, for some reason or another these dreams have died in the hearts of those who once possessed them. Maybe the dream was spoken against, minimalized or ostracized. Perhaps you have waited and waited on God and abandoned your dream because you felt the wait was too long. Maybe the dream that you once possessed has died at the hands of someone you once admired or aspired to be. Your dreams may now lay dormant, in the graveyard of dreams abandoned. Can these dreams live yet again? I say yes, but the choice is yours. Just like Ezekiel surveying the valley of dry bones, the Bible says in Ezekiel 37:1-6:

> *The hand of the Lord was on me, and he brought me out by the Spirit of the Lord and set me in the middle of a valley; it was full of bones. 2 He led me back and forth among them, and I saw a great many bones on the floor of the valley, bones that were very dry. 3 He asked me, "Son of man, can these bones live?"*
> *I said, "Sovereign Lord, you alone know."*
> *4 Then he said to me, "Prophesy to these bones and say to them, 'Dry bones, hear the word of the Lord! 5 This is what the Sovereign Lord says to these bones: I will make breath[a] enter you, and you will come to life. 6 I will attach tendons to you and make flesh come upon you and cover you with skin; I will put breath in you, and you will come to*

life. Then you will know that I am the Lord.'"

God's rhetorical question to him was, "Can these bones live again?" To which Ezekiel responds, "Sovereign LORD, you alone know" (Ezekiel 37:4). Then God told Ezekiel to speak to the dry bones and say, "I will make breath enter you and you will come to life" (Ezekiel 37:5). Then the Bible records an astounding miracle in verses seven through ten:

> *7 So I prophesied as I was commanded. And as I was prophesying, there was a noise, a rattling sound, and the bones came together, bone to bone. 8 I looked, and tendons and flesh appeared on them and skin covered them, but there was no breath in them.*
> *9 Then he said to me, "Prophesy to the breath; prophesy, son of man, and say to it, 'This is what the Sovereign Lord says: Come, breath, from the four winds and breathe into these slain, that they may live.'" 10 So I prophesied as he commanded me, and breath entered them; they came to life and stood up on their feet—a vast army.*

Transposing this to our dreams, God is going to remove the toxic mindset that our dreams will never come to fruition. God wants us to speak life to our dead dreams and carnal mindsets. The power of faith in God's promises is a supernatural element that shatters the voice of doubt and the natural mind which is contrary to the Spirit (Galatians 5:17).

Favored Mindset:
My God-given Dreams Will Come to Pass
in God's Time and in God's Way

When I was about eight years old, I knew I wanted to be a Pastor. My dad was a Pastor, so I was immersed in ministry all my life. As a kid I had big dreams of traveling the world preaching, teaching, and speaking at conferences and seminars. I dreamt of pastoring in a big city. I dreamt of writing books and marrying a beautiful woman.

While I can admit that not all the things I dreamed of happened when I wanted, they still all happened! I have had the privilege of preaching at numerous conferences. I'm a pastor in Los Angeles County, I have written books; and I'm going to write more, I've traveled the world; and I'm going to travel more of the world. But my greatest dream fulfilled is that I'm married to my beautiful wife, Sabrina, who is beautiful both inside and out! She is truly the woman of my dreams. Next year we will be married for twenty years! All my dreams have come to pass in God's time and in God's way. Never in the way that I had hoped or imagined, but I wouldn't trade it for the world.

The million-dollar question many of us are asking is, "how can I make my dreams come to pass?" That is a fallacious question, that is answered with a truthful statement. Which is, God makes our God-given dreams come to pass in His time and in His way. I want to encourage you to trust Him especially in this because it isn't easy. This is what we should do while He's working:

Enjoy the journey. While we are waiting, we should enjoy the journey. Recently, at our Single's Conference a good friend of ours, Mia, shared her story on how she waited for a husband for over eighteen years! She said that instead of always being consumed with getting married, she enjoyed herself in her singleness. She volunteered at the church, traveled, and enjoyed her friendships and ministry. She wasn't out looking for a mate but testified how God brought him to her. Now our friend Mia is happily married to a great man of God, who fully loves God and her! Instead of Mia bitterly waiting impatiently, Mia enjoyed the journey!

Trust in God's Sovereignty. Perhaps God closed a door that you really wanted to be open. What do you do? Do you go knocking on that door over and over? No, the best thing is to move on and trust in God's Sovereignty. We are about to get deep right now. Here we go, are you ready? God knows the very number of hairs on your head. That is profound. God knows the beginning of your life and the end of your life. He knows the limits of your travel, where you would live, and to whom you would be born to. He knows His purpose for your life and whom your life would touch. He holds our breath in His hands, and He will take it from us on a day that only He knows. God is in the details. The God who created the heavens and keeps the sun rising faithful every morning since the beginning of time can be trusted to bring our God-given dreams to fulfillment.

Reflect on God's goodness. While we are on this journey don't become a Christian pessimist. Which I find to be an oxymoron of sorts. Sadly, we have been programmed to overlook the miracles that can be seen through eyes of faith. As believers we are to believe what Scripture says about us. In all the negativity that we are facing, there is always a miracle that we can reflect on and be encouraged by. In every moment there is something that we can be thankful for. Even the small blessings must be reflected on. When reflecting on the sacred writings of the Bible, we see that as believers we are dripping with God's favor.

> *"Glory to God in the highest heaven, and on earth peace to those on whom his favor rests."*
>
> *- Luke 2:14*

"Finally, brothers and sisters, whatever is true, whatever is noble, whatever is right, whatever is pure, whatever is lovely, whatever is admirable-if anything is excellent or praiseworthy—think about such things."

- Philippians 4:8

"I will remember the deeds of the LORD yes; I will remember your miracles of long ago. I will consider all your works and meditate on all your mighty deeds."

- Psalms 77:11-12

Prayer to Revive a God-given Dream

Lord, You are the Dream Giver, and I come to You asking for Your strength and grace in my life. All the God-given dreams that You have planted in my heart- I ask that You bring life to them. Let me not abandon the dreams You gave me because of what others have spoken or even what I have spoken in unbelief. Revive the dreams that have come from Your heart. Let me protect them, fight for them, nurture them, and possess them. When I'm waiting, give me your strength to hold on when I grow impatient. Your Precious Word will sustain me and guide me as I trust in You. Let me speak life to those dreams when others attempt to speak death over them. Let me hold on in patience, fight in faith, and stand tall in hope. Lord You are the Dream Giver, and my eyes will see all my God-given dreams come to pass. All this I ask by faith, in Christ Jesus, Amen.

A Favored Mindset

"We demolish arguments and every pretension that sets itself up against the knowledge of God, and we take captive every thought to make it obedient to Christ."

- 2 Corinthians 10:5

"We cannot change our past... we cannot change the fact that people will act in a certain way. We cannot change the inevitable. The only thing we can do is play on the one string we have, and that is our attitude. I am convinced that life is 10% what happens to me and 90% of how I react to it. And so it is with you... we are in charge of our attitudes."

- Charles R. Swindoll [3]

There was once a gigantic circus elephant confined to an iron beam with a thin rope around its leg. One spectator

[3] http://www.planetofsuccess.com/blog/2019/115-inspirational-change-quotes-to-shift-your-mindset, accessed August 8, 2021

asked the animal's trainer if it was safe because it could easily be snapped by the elephant's sheer strength. He replied, "When the elephant was younger it was tied to a metal chain, and when it tried to escape it couldn't. As the years went by, the elephant became used to being confined. So now, I don't even have to use the iron fetter because the elephant has been trained to believe that it can't escape."

Mindsets matter. The engrained thought patterns that we possess affect us day after day. Just like in the story of the elephant, although his freedom was possible, his mindset was hindered by his past unsuccessful attempts to escape to freedom.

Relating that idea to our own lives, there are many people who, like me, viewed things from a place of pain. I was enslaved to a worldview in which I didn't matter to Christ, thinking He didn't notice me, and that favor was only for His favorites. Thankfully, God's Word gives us simple but profound keys to thinking in spiritual freedom. The thoughts that we mediate on are of utmost importance. The bible even says that our life flows from them (Proverbs 4:23). This freedom is only possible through the power of Christ. His grace makes all things possible. So even if you are in a mental prison, bound to an unbiblical view of your life and world, I confidently proclaim it is for freedom that Christ has set you free (Galatians 5:1).

The foundation in this place is repentance. The Greek word is metanoeó which means "to think differently." In other words, to accept God's will, and to make God's way of thought our way of thought. With this mindset we agree with His laws: acknowledging ourselves as past lawbreakers humbly submitting to the Lawgiver. Biblically speaking, the first step to thinking differently is repentance. This is what metanoeó is all about.

Even if we aren't the worst sinner, we are still sinners (Psalms 14:3). I have that in common with you. I need God's grace and you need God's grace, and the entire population of mankind with every generation from time's past has the same need. Every human since chapter one of Genesis needs God's amazing grace. There hasn't been one who had a perfect mindset with the exception of One. God's Son, Christ Jesus, the epitome of perfection in all directions. His mindset was without spot, solely pure, impeccable throughout life, uncontaminated by the toxins of impure thought patterns handed down from our corrupted linage. Christ broke the curse of misguided mindsets. His death nailed it, and His resurrection from the death confirmed it. Freedom to think like Christ is possible. If we metanoeó, we can have a new mindset; thinking like Him. Wow, what a concept. To have a mindset of the most loving, forgiving, pure, righteous, and humble person to ever live. This is only possible if some misguided mindsets are crucified, and Christ's mindset is cultivated.

Misguided Mindset:
I'm Not Favored by God

Psychologists say we think 6,000 thoughts per day.[4] That's around 2,190,000 thoughts per year, and to think He knows all the thoughts of our total lifetime--all of them! How many of those thoughts are antithetical to the mindset we are to embrace? Lots and lots of them. Naturally, our thoughts are bent on inclinations of evil. The Bible even says in Genesis 6:5, "The Lord saw how great the wickedness of the human race had become on the earth, and that every inclination of the thoughts of the human heart was only evil all the time."

When was the last time we had a sinful thought and allowed it to distract or even hinder us from honoring Christ? If we're honest, probably recently, maybe even today, maybe even within this last hour. This is a battle between our ears that we all have to fight. There are millions of misguided mindsets that are out there, but there are three common thought toxins in all misguided mindsets:

- *I don't need to change*
- *I'm not valuable to God*
- *His favor isn't for me*

Consequently, these mindsets breed rotten fruit in our

---

[4] Jason Murdock, Newsweek, last modified July 15, 2020, https://www.newsweek.com/humans-6000-thoughts-every-day-1517963.

lives. The first one mentioned, "I don't need to change," is particularly detrimental in all aspects of ones' life (Romans 6:23). Living in willful sin will produce all kinds of negative circumstances within our lives. Shame and guilt are two of the many things that living without repentance will create. When we live unrepentant, we sabotage our future (Proverbs 5:22). For example, families are destroyed because one person decided not to follow God's commands found in Scripture. When a husband or wife leaves God, the collateral damage is devasting. Homes are damaged, and hearts are broken. They definitely can be restored if that person repents, but sadly, surrendering to God and repentance isn't always the case. But when it is, God's miracle-working power invades their lives because repentance brings positive breakthrough.

Then there is the mindset that we are not valuable to God. This leads us to doubt His love and question His goodness. Sometimes our situations discourage us, and the mind battles that come our way can make us think that we aren't valuable to God. Or maybe the discouragement comes from the words or actions of people. Perhaps we have been abandoned, hurt, or rejected. The history of certain moments in our lives can make us believe we are not valuable, but that couldn't be further from the truth.

Finally, there is the toxic mindset of believing "His favor isn't for me." We can reason, "I'm not good enough, I don't deserve His favor in my life," or even think the notorious, "I have done too many bad things to ever have favor bestowed upon my life." Looking at all our mistakes and failures could bring us all to the place of utter hopelessness. Once again, we find ourselves in the same boat as everyone else. We are all sinners, in dire need of a remedy. The good news is that we can all fight these mindsets victoriously! Let's look at how God wants us to fight.

Favored Mindset:
I'm Dripping with God's Favor

Having the mind of Christ is a doctrine found in Paul's first letter to the church in Corinth. Chapter 2:16 states, "Who has known the mind of the Lord so as to instruct him?" But we have the mind of Christ. Living according to the Spirit, in step with His will this supernatural mindset is obtainable. Paul confidently writes, we have "the mind of Christ." Although some would argue such a thing impossible, canonical writing points out otherwise. When Christ came, He purposed to break down cognitive ideologies that were contrary to the thoughts of Heaven.

Studying three Greek words found in the New Testament we will discover the keys to see that we are dripping with God's favor. These words are: metanoeó, poiēma, and charis.

We briefly covered how metanoeó, the Greek word for repentance, has transformative power within our lives. Metanoeó crushes the mindset of, "I don't need to change," because without change we are stuck in a cycle of sin. Simply put, God requires that we turn from sin and turn to Him. Acts 3:19 says, "Repent, then, and turn to God, so that your sins may be wiped out, that times of refreshing may come from the Lord." If we metanoeó, we see two amazing benefits in our lives. First, our sins are wiped away. The lawless deeds that we committed are erased from the story in our lives. They are remembered no more. Then secondly, the tonic effect we witness of metanoeó is astounding. We are refreshed, and the sinful clogs in the valves of our hearts are unclogged. The Spirit is given liberty to flow within our lives! The blessing of refreshing comes upon our lives when we repent of our sins.

Looking at the toxin of "I'm not valuable to God" is demolished by a word that is used two times in the New Testament, it's the word poiēma. This word is mentioned in Ephesians 2:10 where Paul writes, "For we are His workmanship, created in Christ Jesus for good works, which God prepared beforehand that we should walk in them." Poiēma is the Greek word for workmanship. It carries a connotation of the God Who holds eternity in the hollows of His hands, Who created the vast oceans, islands, and tropical forests. He is the One Who made the earth, and the heavens, and He is the One Who made you. You have been created by design, with purpose, and for His glory. The profound privilege of being created in the Imago Dei has been entrusted to us (Genesis 1:27).

Lastly, the idea, "God's favor isn't for me," is defeated by the Greek word charis. This word is used for grace. Charis is a word that changed everything, and I mean everything. This is what changes us. By grace we have been saved from our trespasses and sins. The punishment that was coming our way was circumvented by charis. It means something that it's isn't deserved, but it's granted as a gift. When Christ died for our sins, that was charis in action. We don't deserve favor but by God's indescribable charis He has released it to us. Truly, it is the greatest gift ever given to mankind. His grace makes favor possible, and favor is evidence that grace is working within our lives. John 1:16 says, "Out of his fullness we have all received grace in place of grace already given." Truly, metanoeó, poiēma and charis exhibit that we are dripping with God's favor in our lives!

Like the elephant that was mentioned at the beginning of this chapter, there could be an elephant in our life keeping us from walking in the freedom that Christ has given us. Our mindsets can imprison us to believe that freedom isn't possible, and that change is only possible for a few elect. Thankfully, we too can have freedom to walk in God's abundant favor. The power of God is accessible to each of us through Christ Jesus. His finished work on the Cross was the game-changer that ushered us into a new way of thinking: His way of thinking, the mind of Christ. A mindset that favored people possess. Would you humbly join me in a prayer that is written below? This prayer if spoken in faith, can possibly forever change our lives.

Prayer of Favor

Lord, thank You for dying on the Cross for me. You have broken every curse that hung over my life by Your sacrifice on Calvary (Colossians 2:15). Only You are worthy to receive the praise and glory. Your Name is highly exalted in my life. From this day forward I'm going to walk in obedience to Your will and calling for my life. Help me to let go of every belief that hinders me from walking into my destiny. I will repent from every mindset that displeases You. I accept that I'm extremely valuable to You. Your life and sacrifice on the Cross are evidence of this. I know that I'm dripping with Your favor in every area of my life. Lord, right now please give me a new heart and a new mind. By faith in Your promises, I put off ways of thinking that are contrary to Your Word (Philippians 4:8). I put on the helmet of salvation, my thinking will be true, my mediation will be noble, my mindset will be pure, my contemplation will be lovely, if anything is excellent or praiseworthy, I'm going to think on these things! All this I declare in the Mighty Name of Jesus, Amen.

Favored to Forgive

"But Joseph said to them, "Don't be afraid. Am I in the place of God? You intended to harm me, but God intended it for good to accomplish what is now being done, the saving of many lives."

- Genesis 50:19-20

"Forgiveness is the key which unlocks the door of resentment and the handcuffs of hatred. It breaks the chains of bitterness and the shackles of selfishness."[5]

– Corrie Ten Boom

Have you ever been bitten by offense? The venom of offense has struck its fangs in all of us. At home, school, our workplace and sadly, even in ministry. From people we may not have expected it from. People whom we admire, and even love can do things that aren't right. Clearly violations of promises, goodness, and biblical

---

[5] Corrie ten Boom. Clippings from my Notebook. Nashville, Tennessee: Thomas Nelson Inc, 1982.

standards. We can conclude that injustice has robbed our dreams or even destroyed our full potential. The truth is people can't rob your favor unless you let them, and the easiest way to allow this to happen is through unforgiveness.

We have all faced the pain of offense. Like Joseph, who was beaten up by his brothers and had his ornate robe violently ripped off of him. He was then thrown into a dilapidated dusty cistern and sold as a slave to Midianite merchants (Genesis 37:28). Talk about trial after trial and hurt after hurt. To add insult to injury, he was sold as a slave for a meager 20 shekels of silver. Can you imagine the thoughts that flooded Joseph's mind as he traveled to a distant land, away from his father, without the beautiful robe that represented Jacobs' love and favor? Tears must have rolled down from his eyes as he thought about his brothers' jealous rage and injustice. What about the dreams that God gave him? Were they destroyed along with his robe and dignity? No, these offenses were part of God's sovereign plan which would fulfill Joseph's dreams in God's way and in God's time.

There is a battle that wars in the chambers of our hearts. That's why Solomon wrote, "Above all else, guard your heart for everything you do flows from it" (Proverbs 4:23). If we aren't careful, we can subscribe to a mindset that filters everything and everyone from a place of offense and hurt. When offenses come our way, it isn't easy. Our heart can become infected, and our outlook jaded. Negativity is contagious, and it's also hard to get rid of. Once your infected by the disease of bitterness, the only vaccine that can cure us is forgiveness.

Unforgiveness can be deadly.

Dreams die
Vision dies
Strength dies

Misguided Mindset:
I Lose When I Forgive

We can become toxic and driven by offense. Sadly, we can even become motivated by the offense instead of being led by God's love and God's favor. Offense can fuel you forward, but you'll only make it half-way; and it won't be a pleasant journey. Conversely, God's grace and strength will allow you to walk fully into your destiny and enjoy the ride while you get there.

Let me give you an example. I remember after being a pastor for some time, a man who I looked up to for many years made some remarks about me such as, "You don't have what it takes to be successful in ministry." Those words hurt, and for a season, I used them to motivate me forward. I held onto them in a negative way. It was a fuel, but it was a toxic fuel, harmful to the environment that surrounded my life.

Months went by and one day, while I was worshiping God, He spoke to my heart to let go of that offense. He went deep into the chambers of my heart and showered me with His indescribable love. Tears flooded my eyes as Jesus ministered to my heart, with His gentle touch, my Saviors' touch. His love overwhelmed me and reminded me what truly is my motivation. His love is the greatest, and no one can separate us from it (Romans 8: 39). Looking back, if I allowed that offense to fester and didn't release it to God, it would have been a death sentence to my joy, and I would have been oblivious to God's favor over my life.

His love for us leads us to victory, and His love for us leads us to forgive. His love forgave us. His love for us is mighty.

"For as high as the heavens are above the earth, so great is his love for those who fear him; as far as the east is from the west so far has he removed our transgressions from us."
- Psalms 103:11-12

Favored Mindset:
I'm Favored and When I Forgive
God Gets Involved and Handles the Burden
that is Too Heavy for Me to Carry

When we forgive others, it releases us from burdens and weights that we were never intended to carry. We begin to flow in the direction that Christ has called us to. Jesus gave us a beautiful example of forgiveness. The Bible says in Luke 6:37-38, "Do not judge, and you will not be judged. Do not condemn, and you will not be condemned. Forgive, and you will be forgiven. Give, and it will be given to you. A good measure, pressed down, shaken together, and running over, will be poured into your lap. For with the measure you use, it will be measured to you."

This verse shows us to leave our offenses to Jesus and be quick and willing to forgive. Our natural senses tell us to harbor our offenses and to waddle in them, but God's Word shows us a different path: the path to healing. A path of giving forgiveness instead of withholding it.

There are so many benefits that come with forgiveness. One of the greatest is that forgiveness releases us from the burden of retaliation. Many times, when we are hurt by others we want to get even. We might want to get them back in a worse way than they got us. This fleshly and counterintuitive mindset will waste your time, sap your peace, and rob you of your purpose. You won't be dripping with favor, but you'll be tripping with despair. Letting go of the need to get even and releasing the offense at the feet of the Cross is exactly what Joseph did when his father Jacob passed away. This was a time when he could have retaliated against his brothers.

A quick study of the book of Genesis reveals that God

turned things around in favor of Joseph. As we seen in previous chapters, God strategically placed Joseph in places that he didn't want to be, in order to make him the man that God wanted him to become. After Potiphar's house, a cold prison cell, and many years of trusting the Lord, God turned things around in a moment of divine favor.

After successfully interpreting dreams of fellow inmates and the dreams of Pharoah himself, He was elevated to second in command (Genesis 41:41). God began to fulfill the dreams that Joseph dreamt as a teenager. These were dreams of a divine assignment, to save others, and to minister provision. God warned Pharoah through consecutive dreams of an impending famine that was going to ravish the land. Even affecting Josephs' family hundreds of miles away. Disaster was coming and God gave Joseph a plan to prepare for the future food storage. After seven prosperous years, famine struck the whole world, and Josephs' brothers came to Egypt looking for food. The tables had turned. Now Joseph was in a position of leadership, and his brothers were at his mercy. Joseph could have retaliated. He had the chance, but instead he forgave. The Bible even records him saying, "So then, don't be afraid. I will provide for you and your children." And he reassured them and spoke kindly to them (Genesis 50:21).

I'm confident that Joseph wrestled with forgiving his brothers for their injustice, but forgiveness prevailed. He allowed God to bring reconciliation instead of seeking retribution. He told them not to fear and reassured he would provide for their needs and also for the needs of their offspring. Forgiveness is proven by the action that accompanies it. When you're bitten you don't bite back, you bless back! Favor flows from this place.

Furthermore, forgiveness is an act of faith. It is showing--God I trust You. I know that You see, and that You'll never leave me alone even in the midst of the pain. The Bible constantly reassures us that God goes with us, even in the pain. Never will I leave you never will I forsake you (Hebrews 13:5). When we forgive, it strengthens our faith because we are demonstrating by action that we are children of God, and our actions are on display for all to see. Faithlessness is evident by unforgiveness. If we truly believe that God has forgiven us of our sins, we are quick to forgive others. We take His Word for what it is, and if He has given us an example of forgiveness and has commanded us to forgive, then by faith we forgive.

Another benefit of forgiveness is that it allows you to see God's favor in your life. When we are dealing with unforgiveness, we lose sight of what God has done, what He is currently doing, and what He has up ahead. Your vision can be so focused on the offenses that we lose sight of the favor that is resting upon our lives. Case in point, a husband battling bitterness taking out his resentment on his wife and children because the offense consumes his thoughts. Although he loves his family, the root of unforgiveness is filtering out toxins in his life as a husband and as a father. If he allows the Holy Spirit to lead him to forgive, forgiveness will set him free.

Moving from Hurt to Healing

Confession brings healing in our lives. When we confess to God and others that we have allowed unforgiveness in our hearts, God is able to bring healing (James 5:16). When we come to a place of transparency and acknowledge that our heart isn't in a posture of forgiveness, we are opening our hearts to the Lord. Confession realigns our hearts to the Word of God and is step one in following God's direction (Romans 10:10). It shows the Lord that we agree with His Word, and we are walking in obedience to Him.

In the book of Romans, Paul the Apostle tells believers to "bless those who persecute you" (Romans 12:14). Talk about doing something inconvenient. Many times, we need to do the opposite of what we feel, or think is right. Our feelings are bent on unforgiveness, and it's natural to hold on to offenses. Our mind wants to campout where the offense took place and make it our home. No one ever overcame evil by unforgiveness. Evil cannot trump evil. Only good can overcome evil. Forgiveness is good. It's good for you and good for others. When we show kindness to those who hurt us, like Joseph demonstrated to his brothers, the works of the enemy are dismantled, and genuine community occurs.

Lastly, we must seek reconciliation. This profound act promotes unity and honors God. There may be times when we seek to mend a relationship only to be met by rejection. Regardless of what other's may do or not do, God sees the posture of your heart. An olive branch that is not received by man is received by God, and He will honor the hearts of those who seek to be peacemakers. We must be mindful that reconciliation is a ministry that God has entrusted to us. The Bible even says in 2 Corinthians 5:18, "All this is from God, who reconciled us to himself through Christ and gave us the ministry of reconciliation." As we seek reconciliation, the Lord is working behind the scenes on our behalf. What the enemy purposed to divide; God can restore when we choose to forgive. Today, even right now, choose to forgive. Only you can make that decision for yourself. The only thing you lose when you forgive is the burdens that you're carrying.

Prayer of Forgiveness

Lord, thank You for being with me in the hardest times of my life. Even when people, who I trust, commit offenses against me not in line with Your Word. I ask for strength to forgive and not to harbor offense any longer. I desire to forgive the way You forgave me of all my sins and released me of the debt of every lawless act. I also forgive and release all those who have hurt me. I give you my hurts, my resentments, those who have offended me, those who have abandoned me, those who have talked bad about me, those who have lied about me, those who have caused me great harm. Let my thoughts, words and actions testify to this. Lord bless my enemies and bring reconciliation to broken relationships. Help me to honor You and others by cultivating a heart of forgiveness. I lay all offenses done against me at the foot of the Cross. Thank You Jesus for removing these burdens from me. All this I pray in the Name above every name, the precious Name of Jesus, Amen.

Favored to Fast

"If my people, who are called by my name, will humble themselves and pray and seek my face and turn from their wicked ways, then I will hear from heaven, and I will forgive their sin and will heal their land."

- 2 Chronicles 7:14

"Prayer needs fasting for its full and perfect development... Prayer is reaching out after the unseen; fasting is letting go of all that is seen and temporal. Fasting helps express, deepen, confirm the resolution that we are ready to sacrifice anything, even ourselves to attain what we seek for the kingdom of God."

- Andrew Murray[6]

Years ago, I had a dream that I was walking in a dark, gothic city in the middle of the night. This city was shrouded in gloom and the nefarious undercurrent

---

[6] Andrew Murray, With Christ in the School of Prayer. New Kensington, Pennsylvania: Whitaker House, 1981.

that lived there was discerned without a word. As I walked through, I noticed a building that was engulfed in flames. The building that was aflame, penetrated the blackness and attracted people to its light. Droves of people were even walking into the building and making their way within the doors and not being harmed by the flames (Daniel 3:25). The closer I got, I heard a loud angelic voice declare, "This church is a church that fasts. These are a people who consistently fast." This is one dream that I have never forgotten. I definitely sensed the Holy Spirit was leading me to what is required to have a thriving ministry. Remnant Church has embraced a culture of fasting and prayer. For example, we have our church doors open for morning prayer at six in the morning throughout the week, and we have set a precedent to fast on Thursdays until the evening. This simple act has recharged our community, ushered in healing, and ignited divine direction.

Revival chronicled throughout the ages always points to fasting as one of the disciplines that ignites its fire. Church history reveals that when men and women seek the Lord through fasting, a metamorphosis, a breakthrough comes. One example is that of John Wesley, a key figure in the First Great Awaking in America and Britain, who is said to have consistently fasted on Wednesdays and Fridays until the late afternoon for many years. [7]

---

[7] Steven Johnson, The spiritual discipline of Fasting, https://goodnewsmag. org/2012/01/the-spiritual-discipline-of-fasting/, Accessed June 11, 2021.

Misguided Mindset:
I Don't Need to Fast

One thing I can attest to is that fasting isn't easy. Would you agree? This spiritual discipline is hard, and it pushes us to give up feeding our physical appetites and trading our forks and spoons for our Bibles and times of prayer. We lose out on going to our favorite restaurant and enjoying a delectable meal, a savory piece of meat, a juicy cheeseburger, an ice-cold sweet tea, a cheesy cup of your favorite mac and cheese or favorite cup of ice cream.

Fasting puts our carnal nature on notice, and our flesh, when it's not fed, begins to die. This action is very, very, inconvenient and uncomfortable. When our flesh isn't being nourished, it will throw a fit and give you ample reasons not to fast. Headaches, body aches and irritability can occur while toxins are leaving our bodies. The struggle is real. While this battle to crucify our carnal nature is taking place, we are faced with a choice: will we fast, or will we quit? Thankfully, when God leads us to a time of fasting, He will also provide the sustaining grace for us to be victorious.

Favored Mindset:
When Christ Leads Me to Fast,
His Grace will Sustain Me

"When should we fast?" This is a question we may find ourselves asking. If we look at the life of Jesus, he said in Matthew 6:16, "<u>When</u> you fast." Implying fasting should be expected. Jesus' paradigm also denotes that all believers should fast regularly. Below are examples of opportune times we should fast:

- *When you're faced with a big decision*
- *When you need a miracle*
- *When you're empty*
- *When you're sensing spiritual opposition*
- *When you're needing a breakthrough*
- *When the Holy Spirit leads you to fast*

While fasting, times of refreshing and God's favor rests on us. Recently, I woke to get ready for morning prayer at our church and sensed the Holy Spirit leading me to fast. The church was experiencing a time of spiritual attack. We needed God's strength and protection, and I found out later that others in the church were led to fast as well. The Holy Spirit was putting us all on high alert to "watch and pray" (Mark 14:38). Thankfully, we hearkened to His voice. God shielded us, protected us and gave us His grace during that period.

We are in a spiritual battle against a strong enemy who is relentless. The Word of God assures us that we can be confident in God, but that isn't a license to be lazy or naïve. God has given us armor, and we are to wear it. God has also given us weapons, and we are to use them. The Bible says in 2 Corinthians 10:4, "The weapons we fight with are not the weapons of the world. On the contrary, they have divine power to demolish strongholds."

Fasting is a weapon. In God's Chosen Fast, Arthur Wallace writes, "Constantly we are needing revelation concerning the will of God for our lives. We face situations that call for divine wisdom and understanding."[8] When we fast, we spiritually destroy strongholds that the enemy has set up against us. Fasting is a counterattack that gives us breakthrough. There have been times when I have been overwhelmed, and the things I'm supposed to do seem so huge and insurmountable. Life is full of highs and lows mentally. In one moment we are rejoicing, and in the next we could be facing extreme despondence. While fasting, the huge mountains, duties, tough phone calls, and future, changes from being bleak to being a blessing. No mountain is too tall, and no trial is too hopeless when I choose to fast. God is faithful to bring that fresh touch, the Father's touch, when we seek Him through prayer and fasting.

---

[8] Arthur Wallis, God's Chosen Fast. Fort Washington, Pennsylvania: CLC Publications, 1968.

Before you step out on that new venture, before you commit to that new ministry, seek a time of solace with prayer and fasting. God will speak to you and show you the steps to take. Psalms 37:4 declares, "The steps of a good man are ordered by the Lord: and he delighteth in his way." Instead of making a decision on impulse, feelings or fatigue, let's seek God for His insight and be willing to sacrifice to get it. Fasting says to the Lord--I delight in You more than I delight in food, and I'm willing to seek You for direction in my life. This is a fervent demonstration that we love God more than we love anything else.

The Blessings Released When We Fast

In the book of Isaiah, Chapter 58, we see a poignant example of what happens when we choose to fast God's way. The children of Israel were complaining to God that He wasn't aware of their fasting. God reassured them that He was fully cognizant of their days of fasting but corrected them, and revealed they were fasting in a way that wasn't chosen by Him. They were fasting but not in a way that honored God. During the days of fasting, they exploded in frustration, anger and resorted to fault-finding. Instead of looking to God, they were fixated on carnal, earthly things. They complained that God didn't notice their fasting, but God noticed that when they fasted, they were fasting their way. They fasted in a manner that was contrary to His purpose and plan. Transposing this idea to our lives, we can also make the same mistake that the Israelites did. I know personally that I can fast in a way that doesn't honor God. Whether it's taking glory in being noticed by men, or even allowing my irritability to mistreat my family, but acting kind to others in public. God notices pretentiousness, and He is looking at the heart.

There are two categories of fasting shown to us here. Option one is fasting our way and option two is fasting God's way. I want to choose God's chosen way of fasting. Like you, I don't want to waste my sacrifice, and forfeit the blessings that God has in store for my life.

The first blessing found in Isaiah is freedom and deliverance. Isaiah 58:6 says, "Is not this the kind of fasting I have chosen: to loose the chains of injustice and untie the cords of the yoke to set the oppressed free and break every yoke?" When we fast God breaks the chains of the enemy. How many of us want to see a harvest of souls come to Christ? We can all agree that is our desire, but what are we willing to do for that harvest to come to fruition? The Word of God promises that if we fast God is going to set people free in our families and communities.

The next promise we see tied to fasting God's way is fresh ministry. Isaiah 58:7 declares, "Is it not to share your food with the hungry and to provide the poor wanderer with shelter-when you see the naked, to clothe them, and not to turn away from your own flesh and blood?" When ministry becomes trite, and our ax-head becomes dull, fasting re-calibrates us back to the cutting-edge. A fresh anointing is released, and we are dripping with favor. In ministry, we are constantly giving out and if we aren't careful, we can become depleted. Fasting brings freshness. Like a cup of cold mountain water from its spring is to a thirsty soul, is fasting to God's children.

Supernatural healing is the next blessing we witness. Isaiah 58:8 says, "Then your light will break forth like the dawn, and your healing will quickly appear." There are so many people that need healing that only becomes possible by the power of God. When we fast for our loved ones and for those that touch our lives, God sees, and He brings supernatural healing. Marriages are healed, families are restored, and physical infirmities are cured by the supernatural power that comes from Jesus Christ (Hebrews 13:8).

The Blessing of God's Divine Protection is stated in Isaiah 58:8, "Then your righteousness will go before you, and the glory of the LORD will be your rear guard." Fasting works as a shield protecting us in the battle. The protection that God brings to us many times goes unnoticed because the Lord works behind the scenes in the supernatural. Our natural eyes can't see what, when, or why, but our spiritual eyes can discern that He is up to something. The Bible even records a story of a young man who was so fearful of a vast army that had surrounded him and the Prophet Elisha. The terrified man was reassured by Elisha not to fear because they had the angelic support protecting them in the supernatural realm. Elisha said to him, "Do not be afraid, for those who are with us are more than those who are with them" (2 Kings 6:16). Then Elisha prayed that God would open the man's eyes so that he could see God's army protecting him. Finally, this scared man seen that he didn't need to fear; God was working in the unseen realm protecting His people. The same is true for us. We too are being protected by God's army! I remember a time when I felt this protection as a young man driving home from working a graveyard shift. One night, on a two-way road on a country highway, a vehicle from the other lane slipped into my lane. I swerved and lost control of my car, narrowly missing the car that was speeding towards me. My car came to a stop on the side of that rural road in one piece, safe and unharmed. I was definitely shaken up by what took place, but I sensed God's protection over my life.

The next benefit of fasting is answered prayer. Isaiah 58:9 says, "Then you will call, and the LORD will answer; you will cry for help, and he will say: Here am I." When our church just started, we didn't have a facility to call our home. As I mentioned before, we went from a park to a parking lot, and then to a patio area. Talk about a unique journey! Thankfully it was summertime when we started. However, by the time we were at the patio area, it was wintertime and cold. With outside heaters and blankets, it was still cold, and we needed to get indoors. In the beginning of 2021, our church corporately commenced a 21-day Daniel Fast. At the top of our prayer list, was for us to be inside a church with a secure, contractual agreement. We prayed and believed and halfway through the fast we didn't see what we had wanted. I think some of us wrestled with doubt, wondering if we are being noticed in Heaven? At the end of the fast, God provided a home for us, and finally, a contract was signed. The whole church seen that God answers prayers when we fast, and our building is a testament to that reality.

Finally, we will be looking at the blessing of God's direction. Isaiah 58:11 proclaims, "The LORD will guide you always; he will satisfy your needs in a sun-scorched land and will strengthen your frame. You will be like a well-watered garden, like a spring whose waters never fail." When we have choices to make and need direction, fasting is a great way to find the mind of God. There is something that God honors when we lay food aside to seek His direction. There will be times in all of our lives when we have huge decisions to make, and in those moments, we need to allow His will to be accomplished in our lives. Fasting removes the blockage that clogs our heart from hearing God's voice. With no obstructions to battle, we flow smoothly into the will of God. Doors that are not ordained by the Lord will suddenly close, while doors that are part of His perfect will open before our eyes.

We can't afford not to seek God through prayer and fasting. Let us be receptive to His still, small voice from on High when He leads us to commune with Him through fasting. The rewards far exceed the cost. The dividends that come with fasting are an eternal currency which cannot be lost.

A Prayer While Fasting

Lord, thank You for all You have done in my life. Right now, I am seeking You with fasting and prayer. I pray for Your grace to sustain and lead me while I lay food aside to seek You. I repent of anything that dishonors or displeases You within my heart. I turn back to You and fix my eyes on Your perfect will for my life. Not my will, but Your will be done. Strengthen me, equip me, lead me, protect me, shield me, cleanse me, purify me, and mold me, into the vessel that You desire for me to be. You are my joy and delight. To know You is better than life. For in You I have abundant life. In Your Mighty Name, the Name of Jesus I pray, Amen.

God Favors the Humble

"God opposes the proud but shows favor to the humble."

- James 4:6

Humility, that low, sweet root, from which all heavenly virtues shoot.

- Thomas Moore[9]

When I attended my graduation for Bible School, I was so excited to know that Dr. Berin Gilfillan, the founder of the International school of Ministry (ISOM), would be in attendance to hand out diplomas to the graduates. As my family and I drove to the Rock Church in San Bernardino, California for the graduation ceremony, thoughts of seeing fellow students and instructors were racing through my imagination. To also know that Dr. Berin, who envisioned an international Bible School, would be there too, excited me. His God-given vision has literally touched thousands upon thousands of

---

[9] https://www.inc.com/dave-kerpen/15-quotes-that-remind-us-of-the-awesome-power-of-humility.html, accessed August 8, 2021.

people on every continent in the world.

When I arrived for graduate check-in, I noticed among the dozens of graduates, Dr. Gilfillan conversing among us common folks instead of being hidden in a green room in the gigantic facility. With a smile and gentle spirit, he gracefully walked, talked and even was involved in tasks that some may have thought to be marginal for a college president. He assisted with things such as helping move chairs and guiding students to their seats. That day, my life changed. I saw a powerful man, with an immense far-reaching influence, set an example of humility. As he walked through out the stage in front of hundreds of people, I seen a man dripping with God's favor. I knew right then that the God of heaven blesses the humble with His favor.

We are all on a battlefield where pride wants to consume our hearts. Especially, if you dream big dreams of seeing God work in a mighty way through you. As we are on this battleground, we will see successes. With God we will obtain victories. There will be moments when people come up to us and say, "Wow, you did such a great job!" and, "You're so awesome!" and the notorious, "If I could be like you!" All of these statements coupled with our social media craze could produce some narcissistic people. We as children of God must cultivate an attitude of humility. This is counter cultural to the mindset that is saturated in self.

At Remnant Church we are striving to build a culture of humility, where nothing is beyond any of us. For example, you will catch all of us volunteers (first-steps, pastors, worship leaders, creatives) helping with things like welcoming visitors, but also fixing chairs and taking out trash, helping in any way humanly possible. And when we say humanly possible, we mean humanly possible. We serve because we all want to honor God and honor others by living with a spirit of humility. As we study scripture and the person and example of Christ, we see the greatest leader of all-time was the greatest servant of all-time. Nothing is beyond us, so we labor to live like Jesus did, and to follow His perfect example of servanthood.

Misguided Mindset:
I'm Weak When I'm Meek

The world we live in is full of hierarchies and ladders, where meekness is equated with weakness. Those who walk in humility are looked upon as weaklings, lacking the killer instinct in the battle of survival of the fittest. People climb on top of each other, doing whatever, to whomever, to make it to the top. The flawed world's system is consumed with promotion that people think will bring fulfillment and purpose. Some people race to the top to be number one, so they won't have to lift a finger, while still calling the shots from the top, as their peasants do their bidding. Pride pushes people to seek the top so they can be above everyone else. Hopefully, we will never let an attitude like that invade our hearts and attitudes. We all know people who started their careers as the nicest people in the world. Then success comes, and their head starts to swell. They start thinking they are better than others. The venom of pride infects their mindset. They talk to others in a condescending manner, with haughty eyes and pride in their hearts. This is a deadly mixture because pride never produces anything of eternal substance. It kills everything that produces true love and genuine community. If we aren't careful, we can be those people. Pride will want to take over our lives and hearts. We are all susceptible, even the kindest of humanity.

Sadly, and I really mean sadly, the American corporate mindset can even permeate believers to seek promotion and title instead of humility and servanthood. There are people who do what they do to be seen by men, praised by men and elevated by men, instead of being elevated by God, and living a life that is pleasing to God. My encouragement to you is, let God elevate you, because the highest calling is found in being a humble servant to the King of kings. We also must trust that God is the One who exalts a person. 1 Samuel 2:7 says, "The Lord sends poverty and wealth, he humbles, and he exalts." This verse is constant reminder that God lifts up, and He is the One can bring down.

Spiritual ambition could be a great thing in propelling us towards kingdom building, collective edification, and supernatural breakthroughs. This type of ambition is healthy, holy, and wholly centered on the collective good of all. Spiritual ambition changes community, established right relationship, and has everyone's best interest in mind. Growth and spiritual maturity occur when there is spiritual ambition, coupled with humility and self-control. Conversely, selfish ambition is a terrible thing that could turn a saint into a monster. That is why Saint Augustine quipped, "It was pride that changed angels into devils; it is humility that makes men as angels."[10]

The Bible even says in James 3:14-16, "But if you harbor bitter envy and selfish ambition in your hearts, do not boast about it or deny the truth." Such 'wisdom' does not come down from heaven but is earthly, unspiritual, and demonic. For where you have envy and selfish ambition, there you find disorder and every evil practice." This type of ambition is directed inwardly and isn't genuinely concerned about the best interest of others. We can easily read when someone is just in it for themselves. They will use flattery, promise you position, and play on your emotions. But in reality, they are likely using you to get what they desire. Beware, of them and remember the words of Jesus found in Matthew 7:16-20,

By their fruit you will recognize them. Do people pick

---

[10] https://www.brainyquote.com/quotes/saint_augustine_148546, accessed August 9, 2021.

grapes from thornbushes, or figs from thistles? Likewise, every good tree bears good fruit, but a bad tree bears bad fruit. A good tree cannot bear bad fruit, and a bad tree cannot bear good fruit. Every tree that does not bear good fruit is cut down and thrown into the fire. Thus, by their fruit you will recognize them.

A teacher of the word has a huge responsibility in disseminating the gospel with others. If you desire to be a teacher of Bible, you will be a student of the Word, and you will gain valuable knowledge. You will have insight and display the beautiful gems from the treasury of Scripture. There will be moments when you teach, and people will come up to you after and ask you questions. They will seek guidance, wisdom and revelation. They will tell you, "great job!" and, "that was so awesome." You will be driving home, and the enemy of our souls will want you to relish in those words. Pride will try to consume our thoughts and penetrate our heart.

> *Pride is a barrier to all spiritual progress.*
> *- Harry Ironside[11]*

There have been teachers and preachers who fell into pride because they allowed their egos and the limelight to control their thoughts. They have reasoned that they didn't need accountability; they didn't need others to speak into their lives, and they didn't need personal

---

[11] https://www.christianquotes.info/quotes-by-topic/quotes-about-pride/, accessed August 8, 2021.

boundaries. Some have even lost their ministry and influence because they allowed pride to go unabated. Spiritual pride is the hardest to deal with. It argues against safeguards that were indented to protect us not harm us. It's subtle, deceiving and blinding. In our lives we can come to place where we think we are the only ones that hear from God, and that we are His favorite. Although we are favored, we aren't God's favorite, and although we hear from God, we aren't the only ones that God speaks to. Spiritual pride makes us uncorrectable; we can't receive direction from others, and we are disrespectful to others God has gifted. In the Old Testament, we read about a mighty king who was innovative, wealthy, and a great leader. His name was King Uzziah, and in his military, his mighty army experienced success after success, until his heart was lifted up in pride. In 2 Chronicles 26:16-20 the Bibles says:

> But after Uzziah became powerful, his pride led to his downfall. He was unfaithful to the Lord his God and entered the temple of the Lord to burn incense on the altar of incense. Azariah the priest with eighty other courageous priests of the Lord followed him in. They confronted King Uzziah and said, "It is not right for you, Uzziah, to burn incense to the Lord. That is for the priests, the descendants of Aaron, who have been consecrated to burn incense. Leave the

sanctuary, for you have been unfaithful; and you will not be honored by the Lord God." Uzziah, who had a censer in his hand ready to burn incense, became angry. While he was raging at the priests in their presence before the incense altar in the Lord's temple, leprosy broke out on his forehead. When Azariah the chief priest and all the other priests looked at him, they saw that he had leprosy on his forehead, so they hurried him out. Indeed, he himself was eager to leave, because the Lord had afflicted him.

This is such a sad story of how pride's trajectory is always downward. This is ironic because people with pride are attempting to go upward. Uzziah's life is a testament that proud people are not able to receive direction from others. Just as the priest confronted him, Uzziah instead of receiving their commands in meekness, became angry and began raging and insulting the priest. While he did this, leprosy broke out on his face. From that moment until his death, a once prestigious king became a leprous outcast. Pride always destroys, and the epic fall of King Uzziah is evidence of that.

The bible has so much to say about pride and what it does to us, below are a few examples found in the book of Proverbs:

"When pride comes, then comes disgrace, but with humility comes wisdom."

- Proverbs 11:2

"Before a downfall the heart is haughty, but humility comes before honor."

- Proverbs 18:12

"Pride brings a person low, but the lowly in spirit gain honor."

- Proverbs 29:23

We see from the verses above that pride brings disgrace, a downfall and brings us low. We must have confidence that meekness isn't weakness. But rather it shows true strength and confidence in Christ.

Favored Mindset:
I'm Favored When I Walk in Humility

In Remnant Church we have adopted a mindset of meekness. This flows from a servant's heart. There is no greater honor than to have the title of a faithful servant. These are the words, found in Matthew 25:21, that we should all long to hear when we stand before the Lord and give an account of our lives, "Well done, good and faithful servant! You have been faithful with a few things;

I will put you in charge of many things. Come and share your master's happiness!" Those words should be our goal and desire. When these words are our priority, we will strive to walk in humility and set an example of servanthood all the days that God has entrusted to our care. Paul reminds us to walk in humility when he writes under the inspiration of the Holy Spirit,

> *"Be completely humble and gentle; be patient, bearing with one another in love."*
>
> *- Ephesians 4:2*

Paul knew having a mindset of Jesus Christ was a significant aspect in kingdom building. Humility keeps us united. It's the glue that connects all our relationships together. Paul again writes to the church in Philippi,

> *Do nothing out of selfish ambition or vain conceit. Rather, in humility value others above yourselves, not looking to your own interests but each of you to the interests of the others. In your relationships with one another, have the same mindset as Christ Jesus: Who, being in very nature god, did not consider equality with God something to be used to his own advantage; rather, he made himself nothing by taking the very nature of a servant, being made in human likeness. And being found in appearance as a man, he humbled himself by becoming obedient to death—even death on a cross!*
>
> *- Philippians 2:3-8*

From these verses we have a paradigm to follow: the Christ mindset. I conclude this idea with four major points in obtaining this supernatural mindset.

Do nothing out of selfish ambition, or vain conceit. Selfish ambition can be understood as "motivation to elevate oneself or to put one's own interests before another's." It is a self-above-others approach. The Greek term here carries with it a connotation of contentiousness. In fact, the King James Bible translates the word as "strife." Vain conceit means "excessive pride" or, "self-esteem that has no foundation in reality." Vain conceit is an elevated and incorrect sense of self. Therefore, doing nothing out of selfish ambition or vain conceit means not letting our actions be motivated by selfishness, pride, or one-upmanship.[12] Christ didn't do anything to be seen by others. On many occurrences, He could have capitalized on miracles, but He didn't. One example of that is found in John 6:10-14. Jesus said:

> Have the people sit down." There was plenty of grass in that place, and they sat down (about five thousand men were there). Jesus then took the loaves, gave thanks, and distributed to those who were seated as much as they wanted. He did the same with the fish. When they had all had enough to eat, he said to his disciples, "Gather the pieces that are

[12] https://www.gotquestions.org/selfish-ambition-vain-conceit.html, accessed August 9, 2021.

left over. Let nothing be wasted." 13 So they gathered them and filled twelve baskets with the pieces of the five barley loaves left over by those who had eaten. After the people saw the sign Jesus performed, they began to say, "Surely this is the Prophet who is to come into the world." 15 Jesus, knowing that they intended to come and make him king by force, withdrew again to a mountain by himself.

In this portion of scripture, the people wanted to make Jesus the king by force, but instead Jesus chose to slip away to the mountainside to spend time with the Father. Jesus' example was not one of vain conceit. Jesus wasn't trying to be noticed, and He didn't care if He was noticed or not. Jesus' mindset did not want to be a king according to the people's flawed systems. He wasn't needing their approval, or validation. Jesus didn't suffer from an identity crisis. He knew that He was loved, and that the Father had Him on a mission. He recognized he didn't need man's stamp of approval to accomplish that mission.

In humility value others above yourself. Jesus valued others above himself. One great example of this is after the Passover supper. Instead of having Peter, Andrew, and John wash His feet, He humbly washed His disciples' feet. Our Lord girded Himself and washed the feet of his disciples. At this time, Jesus knew that His time was quickly approaching, yet He put that aside and gives us an example of putting others ahead of ourselves. John 13:12-17 says:

> *When he had finished washing their feet, he put on his clothes and returned to his place. "Do you understand what I have done for you?" he asked them. "You call me 'Teacher' and 'Lord,' and rightly so, for that is what I am. Now that I, your Lord and Teacher, have washed your feet, you also should wash one another's feet. I have set you an example that you should do as I have done for you. Very truly I tell you, no servant is greater than his master, nor is a messenger greater than the one who sent him. Now that you know these things, you will be blessed if you do them.*

We see that in washing the disciples' feet, Jesus told us to wash one another's feet! Truly an amazing example from our Lord. We are called upon to wash each other's feet, to live in humility and to serve in humility. This is our greatest, purest, and finest example of what it is to be a leader after God's heart.

Not looking to your own interests, but to the interests of the others. Jesus gives us a profound example on placing the interest of others above our own. When Jesus healed the sick after John was beheaded, the Bible records in Matthew 14:12-14,

John's disciples came and took his body and buried it. Then they went and told Jesus.13 When Jesus heard what had happened, he withdrew by boat privately to a solitary place. Hearing of this, the crowds followed him on foot from the towns. When Jesus landed and saw a large crowd, he had compassion on them and healed their sick.

At this moment, Jesus was deeply saddened by John's unjust death. An innocent man, whom He loved and grew up with was now dead. Yet, instead of taking a six-month sabbatical in the Judean desert country club, He chose to put the people above Himself. He ministered, He healed, He fed, He taught, and He loved. When we find ourselves going through the darkest moments of our lives, let us follow the example of Jesus. Let us put the interests of others above ourselves.

He made himself nothing. Jesus made Himself of no reputation. He didn't publish His healing crusades in the "Hebrew Times." His cup wasn't full of Himself. His ambition was pure. His heart was set not on His will, but on the Father's will. Jesus--the Ultimate, the Healer, the King of kings, The Alpha and the Omega, The First and the Last, The Lion of the tribe of Judah, The Fortress, Our Redeemer, Our Refuge, Our Strength, Our Living Hope, The Amen, The Bright Morning Star, The Lily of the Valley. He made Himself of no reputation. This is mind boggling! Throughout history there have been people who have experienced fame, wealth and prestige. They have contentiously fought to have their names remembered on marble stone, in hopes of making an indelible mark in history to not be forgotten. One hundred years after we die, our accomplishments, our accolades and our achievements will be forgotten on this earth. Everything done to be seen by men will not be carried to heaven. Yet it is our good deeds, unseen and unmentioned, that we transport to heaven. The deeds that are done for an audience of One. This is only possible though when we make ourselves nothing. When live as nothing, we are seen in heaven. For example, not caring who gets the credit on a project; or giving up a speaking engagement so another person could develop their gifting and walk in their anointing; or delegating authority, and letting others lead, grow, and develop; being there beside them, and then releasing them into their destiny. We are not graded on how many are under us, but we are blessed by who we teach, equip, and release. John Wesley penned this weighty covenant with God that reminds us that we must make ourselves of no reputation. He writes:

> *"I am no longer my own, but thine. Put me to what thou wilt, rank me with whom thou wilt. Put me to doing, put me to suffering. Let me be employed by thee or laid aside for thee, exalted for thee or brought low for thee. Let me be full, let me be empty. Let me have all things, let me have nothing. I freely and heartily yield all things to thy pleasure and*

disposal. And now, O glorious and blessed God, Father, Son, and Holy Spirit, thou art mine, and I am thine. So be it. And the covenant which I have made on earth, let it be ratified in heaven. Amen."[13]

Truly, that prayer isn't for the faint of heart and should be spoken carefully. The man who wrote that prayer seen the hand of God use him in a mighty wave of revival throughout Europe and America. John Wesley, the founder of the Methodist Church, planted churches all throughout the globe. God was able to use this vessel because he was emptied of himself. When we are used by God, there will be moments when we feel burdened and pressured and may want to give up. In those times we need to spend time alone with our King and receive His rest. In Matthew 11:28-30, Jesus says to us,

"Come to me, all you who are weary and burdened, and I will give you rest. Take my yoke upon you and learn from me, for I am gentle and humble in heart, and you will find rest for your souls. For my yoke is easy and my burden is light."

The strongest leader ever to walk the face of the earth was meek. He was humble, and He was gentle. He promises if we live as He did, we too will find rest for our souls. Let's be humble.

---

[13] https://www.umcdiscipleship.org/blog/the-wesley-covenant-prayer-and-the-baptismal-covenant, accessed, August 9, 2021.

A Prayer for Humility

Lord thank You for allowing me the privilege to serve in Your kingdom for Your glory. When successes and blessings come my way, please let me keep a humble heart and cultivate a contrite spirit. I ask that pride, arrogance, and haughtiness be kept far from my heart and thoughts. You deserve all the Glory and all the honor; it belongs solely to You and You alone. Let me give every victory back to You, laying every crown at the feet of Jesus. Let me walk with a servants' heart and follow Your example that You displayed to us; one of servanthood, genuine love, and putting others ahead of ourselves. All this I ask in Jesus Mighty Name, Amen.

Favored with Provision

"So Abraham called that place The Lord Will Provide. And to this day it is said, "On the mountain of the Lord it will be provided."
- Genesis 22:14

"Where God guides, He provides"

When we first started meeting in the park, we just gathered to worship and pray. The people kept coming, and we knew that we should start a church. So we did what all churches do, we picked up an offering. Thankfully, people gave. A true a miracle. Their generosity will never be forgotten. After the service someone handed me some money for the offering, so my wife and I went to the back of the park where a team of volunteers were counting the donations that were received in the collection. I handed the money to the team and they tallied what came in and it totaled $1,982. I looked at my wife astounded. And I asked, "did you say $1,982?" And to our amazement they said, yes. I started to laugh because my wife and I were born in the great year of 1982. Everyone started to laugh in sheer joy. I looked at this as a sign from above that God was going to provide for the Remnant Church of Whittier, and He has been faithful to all His promises. He is Jehovah Jireh!

Just weeks before this had transpired, I had lost my job. My wife and I were left with a small savings that took us years to save. I remember as I took my letter of termination home, and I laid on my bed in shock, hundreds of thoughts raced through my mind. Thoughts like, "how in the world am I going to provide for four teenagers and my wife," and "how am I going to pay my bills and my rent," and, "was it You Lord that led me to uproot from my church in Visalia?" and, "why is this happening to us?" and, "Lord, what should I do next?" I laid there looking at the ceiling wondering if I made a mistake in moving to Whittier, California, three years earlier. I remember it being a clear, "yes," to move. But now, I started to wonder, if I was hearing right. Have you ever had one of those moments, when your circumstances don't add up to the confirmation that you received from the Lord?

As I laid, I began scrolling at pictures on my phone, pictures from the last three years, pictures of good memories, with my family and my church family. As I scrolled, I began to weep, and I mean cry like I have never cried before. From the depths of my soul, I was weeping. My daughter walked in, and I just kept on crying. I couldn't compose myself. It was a moment I will never forget. The reason is because God met me in this time like never before. He was there in the midst of my fear, in the midst of my brokenness, in the midst of my pain, and in the midst of my "Why God?"

His perfect peace invaded my room, and His tender touch overshadowed my anxiety. He showed me that day that I had nothing to fear when He's leading. He also confirmed to me that my job is only a conduit of His provision, but ultimately everything comes from His hand. He is Jehovah Jireh.

A few days later I received a check in the mail with a generous amount! Then someone paid for my kids' school tuition for the whole school year. People bought us groceries, blessed us with finances, and others gave us powerful words of encouragement and confirmation. And the list goes on and on. My family is more blessed now then we have ever been. A sincere thank you to all that came alongside us in our time of need. You know exactly who you are.

I know that some people feel uncomfortable with me being so transparent about the gifts that people blessed my family with. I understand I have been in church all my life. Throughout the years I've encountered people who have wanted to keep their blessings undercover in fear that people would stop giving. Well, I have found that people who don't want to give, won't give anyways, and a good majority of those who give already, will be proud that God is providing for their pastor and his family. Most generous people welcome seeing others blessed. It's a "poverty" mentality that is pleased to see others lacking. My "boastamony" was just an acknowledgment of God's faithfulness. I won't hide it or deny it. God showed us that He is our Provider. All throughout my years He has been faithful to meet every need. But the miracles He did in 2020 will forever be on the forefront of my heart.

Not only did God provide for me and my family, but our church family at Remnant witnessed people get blessed with new jobs, financial breakthroughs, checks in the mail, and job promotions. Many of our members are entrepreneurs which is an awesome thing to see them prosper in their creativity, innovation and calling. At Remnant Church we foster a heart of generosity where it's giving back to our community, to world missions, investing in our youth and even in our serve teams. We are able to do this because we have people who give of their time, resources, energy and finances.

When I was a teenager, I went to work for my dad. I believe he promised to pay me $300. My plan was to use it to go buy myself some new clothes before a church conference. When my dad paid me, I noticed that 10 percent was missing. I inquired and told dad that money was missing, and to which he said, "I took the tithe out for you." That set me on a journey of giving my tithes to the Lord. I was about 14 or 15 years old when that transpired, but I'm so thankful for it. We have been privileged to trust God with all the income that God has allowed us to be stewards over. In our giving, we have never given to a church or a person. Our giving has flowed from our heart solely for Him. Giving back to Him the tithe for the furtherance and expansion of His Kingdom has been a great honor.

The tithe and offering have taught my wife and I to be stewards over every penny that comes in our care. We look at this as obedience to God's Word. At Remnant we encourage our members to give of their tithes and offering too. Thankfully, with the tithes that have come in, we have been able to pay for a sound system, video system, new chairs for our worship center, missions, community involvement, and church planting. For example, after nine months, we sensed that God was leading us to plant a church in the San Gabriel area of Southern California. After much prayer and times of seeking the Lord through fasting and seeking godly counsel from S.H.I.F.T. Ministries, God opened doors for us to plant our first church in the city of West Covina, California! This was after our church was in existence for only nine months. The irony is that most pregnancy durations is a little over nine months as well. This is a breathtaking testament to the power of a God-given dream giving birth. We were able to make a financial pledge in which we donated an initial $5,000 gift for church planting fees. We are also fully covering the building cost for the first six months, and then half of those costs until the end of the first year. The tithes and offerings that have come in have made this possible. This is a pledge that we are going to make for all of the churches that are sent from Remnant Whittier. Interestingly, the Bible says in Malachi 3:8-12,

> "Will a mere mortal rob God? Yet you rob me. "But you ask, 'How are we robbing you?' "In tithes and offerings. You are under a curse—your whole nation—because you are robbing me. Bring the whole tithe into the storehouse, that there may be food in my house. Test me in this," says the Lord Almighty, "and see if I will not throw open the floodgates of heaven and pour out so much blessing that there will not be room enough to store it. I will prevent pests from devouring your crops, and the vines in your fields will not drop their fruit before it is ripe," says the Lord Almighty. "Then all the nations will call you blessed, for yours will be a delightful land," says the Lord Almighty."

These promises found in Malachi have been apparent in the life of our church. We have seen God open the floodgates of heaven and pour out so many blessings. One of the greatest laws of the Kingdom of God is giving and stewardship. It is a spiritual principle that recognizes God as the Owner and Lord of all things (Psalms 24:1; Colossians 1:17), and it shows to us that we will be held responsible for what God has entrusted to our care. One study mentioned that tithers make up only 10-25 percent of a normal congregation. Only 5 percent of the U.S. tithes, with 80 percent of Americans only giving 2 percent of their income. Christians today are only giving at a 2.5 percent per capita, while during the Great Depression they gave at a 3.3 percent rate. If believers were to increase their giving to a minimum of 10 percent, there would be an additional $165 billion for churches to use and distribute. The global impact would be phenomenal. Here's just a few things the Church could do with the kind of money: $25 billion could relieve global hunger, aiding in the relief of starvation and deaths from preventable diseases in five years. $1 billion could fully fund all overseas mission work. $100 – $110 billion would still be left over for additional ministry expansion.[14] If those numbers are correct, and if the money is stewarded righteously, tithing would change the landscape of the world. There would be no hunger, no lack, and no financial need for the poor. All the needs of the downtrodden and outcast would be met. There would be numerous orphanages for the fatherless and motherless. Human trafficking would be abolished by safe houses, Christian education, financial security, and reliable health care.

---

[14] Mike Holmes, "What would happen if the church Tithed," Relevant Magazine, March 8, 2016, www.revantmagazine.com.

The principle of giving is a biblical truth which brings breakthrough and meets the needs of those who are up against a tough time. The Acts of the Apostles lived in this realm. The Bible says this, in Acts 4:32-35,

> *"All the believers were one in heart and mind. No one claimed that any of their possessions was their own, but they shared everything they had. With great power the apostles continued to testify to the resurrection of the Lord Jesus. And God's grace was so powerfully at work in them all that there were no needy persons among them. For from time to time those who owned land or houses sold them, brought the money from the sales and put it at the apostles' feet, and it was distributed to anyone who had need."*

This example of selfless giving brought about a change in their culture. During these days people were left to fend for themselves. The government of the day didn't provide for the needs of the people. If they didn't have a good harvest, they would be stuck between a rock and a hard place. In the book of Acts, we see the heart of the Father, His way to meet the need of others. I love how there was no needy person among them. The needs of the people were met by the church coming together in one heart, God's heart.

In our city there are many homeless people. During

Thanksgiving time in 2020, a church member had an idea to go to the downtrodden areas and feed the homeless and provided them with the necessitates that they needed. With help of so many of our volunteers and a local BBQ catering business, Crazy Matt's BBQ, we made over one hundred BBQ plates and care packages to share with our friends who were up against some hard times. All the food was completely donated from Crazy Matt's BBQ! Some volunteers brought waters, others brought blankets, others brought Bibles, and the list went on and on. That day was special because we couldn't have done it alone. It only happened because of unity. If any one of us tried to do that by ourselves we would have failed miserably. That is why God designed us to live in unity. More is accomplished as a team and very little can be accomplished alone. God's anointing flows when we are together in generosity. He uses us, corporately, collectively, and collaboratively.

We have all experienced times of abundance and overflow. We know how we were refreshed by our giving. Proverbs 11:24-25 says,

> *"One person gives freely, yet gains even more; another withholds unduly, but comes to poverty. A generous person will prosper; whoever refreshes others will be refreshed."*

Living in generosity is prosperous living. Conversely, there has been times when we faced an unforeseen occurrence such as a loss of a job, the death of a loved one, or an accident that we didn't expect to happen. We have all been there. We have all experienced times when we needed help from our sisters, mothers, brothers and fathers who are part of the body of Christ. As they came to our aid, we witnessed that our generosity was reciprocated. In those moments of trusting God, we have seen that God is faithful to His Word and His name, Jehovah Jireh. When the people of God come to together to give, supernatural miracles happen. In this place of community there is no lack, and there is no need.

Misguided Mindset:
I'm Broke and Can't Give

The enemy will always tell us that we are too broke to give. He will have us looking at our bills, looking at our hourly rate, and looking at our favorite online shopping sites. The enemy will even tell us that our giving doesn't make a difference, and that it doesn't matter if we give or not.

Fear is another culprit that hinders us from stepping out and giving by faith. There are many who want to give but fear stops them from doing so. The fear of lack will attack our faith. No one wants to be unable to provide for their family and others. When I first got married, and my wife and I started to build a family, there were definitely times when it was tempting to hold back and not give. Bills were coming, we needed clothes for the kids, and costs became more expensive as they got older. By the grace of God, we continued to live a life of generosity. Today we are so blessed, and we are glad that fear didn't stop us from giving. The Bible says, "For God has not given us a spirit of fear and timidity, but of power, love, and self-discipline" (2 Timothy 1:7). Fear is a spirit, and spirits are defeated by the power of Jesus Christ. There is no other way that we truly experience freedom in any area of lives. God has promised to give us power, love, and self-control in every area of lives. This includes the area of giving.

Selfishness will keep us from giving to anyone but ourselves. Naturally we are all bent on selfishness. Taking care of me and mine is a mindset that the world has. It was passed on to us by the world's culture, and possibly from our own family. Some may think that we are crazy to give. Others may laugh at us because of their selfish outlook, despising our generous spirit. The best antidote to selfishness is selfless giving. When we give, the toxins of selfishness are destroyed. At first, it's going to hurt, but Scripture encourages us to live a life of generosity. Let's look at the benefits of spirit-filled giving.

Favored Mindset:
I'm Blessed and Ready to Give

Let's just look at the obvious--we are blessed! If we live in the United States of America, we are very fortunate in comparison to the rest of the world. A couple of years ago, the Washington Post in regard to this point stated, "The average U.S. resident estimated that the global median individual income is about $20,000 a year. In fact, the real answer is about a tenth of that figure: roughly $2,100 per year. Similarly, Americans typically place themselves in the top 37 percent of the world's income distribution. However, the vast majority of U.S. residents rank comfortably in the top 10 percent."[15] Whether you know it or not, you are blessed. This is a mindset that is found when we repent from our sins and trust Jesus as our Lord and Savior. Truly a gift that we can never forget or look down upon. With that established, we move on to walking in step with the Spirit. We are given a beautiful illustration of giving from the Apostle Paul. Look with me at 2 Corinthians 9:6-8,

> *"Remember this: Whoever sows sparingly will also reap sparingly, and whoever sows generously will also reap generously. Each of you should give what you have decided in your heart to give, not reluctantly or under*

[15] https://www.washingtonpost.com/news/monkey-cage/wp/2018/08/23/most-americans-vastly-underestimate-how-rich-they-are-compared-with-the-rest-of-the-world-does-it-matter/, accessed August 9, 2021.

compulsion, for God loves a cheerful giver. And God is able to bless you abundantly, so that in all things at all times, having all that you need, you will abound in every good work."

Spirit-filled giving is generous. Paul says, those who sow sparingly will reap sparingly. It's interesting he mentions this because you might conclude that if sow sparingly, you still might reap bountifully. Nope, there is an order given. The more we give, the more that God pours back into our lives. He is generous, more generous than any of us could ever be. We can never outgive the extravagant Giver.

Spirit-filled giving isn't reluctant or compulsive. Then Paul says give what you have decided in your heart. The Holy Spirit will lead us in the area of giving. This takes place in our hearts. Paul says not to give reluctantly or under compulsion. This shows us that we have to be careful not to pressure people to give, or "guilt trip" them into giving. Letting the Spirit touch people's hearts is God's way of doing things. It also shows that the posture of our hearts matters in the area of giving. If we aren't wanting to give, it would be good to examine why we feel this way. Are we afraid? Do we have any walls or restraints? Do we have trust issues? Is the enemy lying to us?

Spirit-filled giving is hilarious. The Greek word for cheerful is hileos, and it's where we get the word hilarious from. Hileos giving is hilarious generosity. We are joyful, we are laughing, we are thankful because we are confident that God will provide for everyone's needs, and more importantly, we're thankful for the privilege to be able to give to the God of Heaven. This can also include the needs of our church. We pray that God would touch all of our hearts to give cheerfully. God loves when His children give hilariously, with joy, with confidence, and with excitement. When this happens, we see the blessings of God flowing. He provides, even when it seems that we won't have enough, but there is overflow, there is abundance, there is more than enough because we serve Jehovah Jireh. This happens all the time. All the needs that we have are met. God will give us provision for the vision.

Furthermore, 2 Corinthians 9:10-11 states,

> *"Now he who supplies seed to the sower and bread for food will also supply and increase your store of seed and will enlarge the harvest of your righteousness. You will be enriched in every way so that you can be generous on every occasion, and through us your generosity will result in thanksgiving to God."*

Spirit-filled giving is multi-harvested. God will increase our seed. Seed represents the substance and wealth that God has entrusted to our care. Visualize a farmer who is planting seeds of corn. The more seeds that he sows, the greater the harvest of corn will he receive. God brings increase and He is the one who enlarges the harvest. We reap blessings when we give in multi-harvests in our lives. The harvest of our righteousness, the harvest of our finances, the harvest of our relationships, and the harvest of our ministries. Not only will our generosity touch our lives, but it will result in thanksgiving to God. That means that others will be impacted by our generosity, and they will give glory and thanksgiving to God because of what you sowed into the kingdom. For example, our church sends $500 a month to help support a group of churches in Africa. We know that those funds are used to build God's kingdom and that the people in Africa are so thankful for those donations. It's resulting in thanksgiving to God.

Spirt-filled giving is sacrificial. Another example of Spirit-filled giving is Barnabas in the book of Acts. The Bible says in Acts 4:36-37, Joseph, a Levite from Cyprus, whom the apostles called Barnabas (which means "son of encouragement"), sold a field he owned and brought the money and put it at the apostles' feet. This was a sacrificial gift. Imagine owning a house, then one morning the Holy Spirit speaking to you to sell your house and give the proceeds to the elders of your church. Talk about a huge gift. He placed his financial security at the feet of the Apostles. Interestingly, he didn't just give 10 percent of the proceeds, he gave it all! I really believe that New Testament giving goes beyond 10 percent. It's lavish, it's sacrificial, and it's without limits. Barnabas gave beyond the status quo. He gave extravagantly.

Spirit-filled giving is intentional. Paul penned these instructions to the church in Corinth, "Now about the collection for the Lord's people: Do what I told the Galatian churches to do. On the first day of every week, each one of you should set aside a sum of money in keeping with your income, saving it up, so that when I come no collections will have to be made" (1 Corinthians 16:1-2). We are to be deliberate when we give. Being consistent and intentional is fruit of wise stewardship. If we are haphazard in our giving, there will be disorder in every other area of our lives. God is organized, deliberate, and intentional. As His children, we should follow His lead.

My life hasn't been the same since that fateful morning at the park with the Remnant financial stewardship team, as they added up $1,982 from the offering. I'm reminded that God is Jehovah Jireh, who faithfully provides for His children and for those who do His glorious work here on earth. And yes, 1982 was a good year!

Prayer for Provision

Lord, thank You for being Jehovah Jireh. I trust You alone for provision and that all my financial needs will be met. I will honor you with tithe and offerings. As Your Word commands us to honor You with our wealth, and with "the first fruits of all our crops; our barns will be overflowing, our vats will brim over with new wine." Let me live with a spirit of generosity, living to refresh others, with an open hand of liberality. Let me give to You in secret, trusting fully that You see every sacrifice and that You only can reward my sacrifice. Help me to be a wise steward, receptive to Your voice, in step with Your Spirit. You are faithful to provide, You supply all my needs, You only are Jehovah Jireh. All this I ask in the glorious Name of Jesus, Amen.

United by Favor

"Therefore I, the prisoner in the Lord, urge you to walk worthy of the calling you have received, with all humility and gentleness, with patience, bearing with one another in love, making every effort to keep the unity of the Spirit through the bond of peace. There is one body and one Spirit—just as you were called to one hope at your calling— one Lord, one faith, one baptism, one God and Father of all, who is above all and through all and in all."

- Ephesians 4:1-6 CSB

Satan always hates Christian fellowship; it is his policy to keep Christians apart. Anything which can divide saints from one another he delights in. Since union is strength, he does his best to promote separation.

- Charles Spurgeon [16]

---

[16] https://www.christianquotes.info/quotes-by-topic/quotes-about-unity/, accessed July 15, 2021.

The beauty of the Remnant Church of Whittier is the different age groups working together as one; multi-generations united as one. Seeing all the different age groups striving for unity is truly a miracle. When challenges come up that want to disrupt our cohesiveness as a unified team, the key ingredients of humility, servanthood and love keep us glued together. This is only possible by the grace of God. He gets all the credit for the work He is accomplishing in His people.

In the scripture text from above, the Greek word for endeavoring is spoudázō — which means to move speedily by showing full diligence to accomplish all that God assigns through faith. It means to not waste any time, and to be swift in the right direction.

Unity isn't easy to foster. It means biting your tongue, overlooking an insult, and being the bigger person in a world when so many people don't want to be. Unity means putting your pride aside for the greater good of the community and the bond of fellowship. It requires us to die to our egos and let God do the work that only He can do.

On the other hand, discord is simple, and it doesn't take any effort. It comes naturally when we let our egos control our heart and tongue. Dissention is the natural result of a fleshy life. Walking in the flesh will produce the fruit of the flesh, and division is one of those fruits. Without endeavoring to keep the unity, division just happens. Nothing of eternal value is accomplished because division kills the vision.

Misguided Mindset:
I Don't Need to be United with Others
in the Body of Christ

In 1 Corinthians 1:10-13, Paul makes his famous plea for division to end when he writes,

> *"I appeal to you, brothers and sisters, in the name of our Lord Jesus Christ, that all of you agree with one another in what you say and that there be no divisions among you, but that you be perfectly united in mind and thought. My brothers and sisters, some from Chloe's household have informed me that there are quarrels among you. What I mean is this: One of you says, "I follow Paul"; another, "I follow Apollos"; another, "I follow Cephas"; still another, "I follow Christ." Is Christ divided? Was Paul crucified for you? Were you baptized in the name of Paul?"*

Apparently, the church in Corinth was suffering from factions among the brethren. One group claimed they followed one person, and another group followed another leader, and finally the last group said that followed Christ. The last group is the one that got it right. Their example is the one that we should follow. In the church today, we can be just like them, choosing sides, favoring one group instead of another, and having our eyes fixated on man or the name of an organization instead of having our eyes on Christ. Below are a couple of ways this happens:

Branding is a huge thing in our culture today. This could be used in a positive way, as it's an effective way in building a platform and sharing your core beliefs with your community and the world. One of the challenges that we can all face is allowing the brand to create a competitive spirit within our communities. Sadly, some could focus too much on the church name, instead of Kingdom building. We are to partner with others in building God's kingdom, not our own kingdoms. We can be competitive, but our competition should be against the kingdom of darkness.

The gang culture for decades has permeated an environment of division. Countless deaths have resulted from a gang's preferred color of clothes, street names, and areas where one has embraced as their hood. The enemy desires that churches, like gangs, fight against each other. "Set tripping" and "spiritual assassination" of other's ministries and character is the highest priority when we have this mindset. This is because division is a work of the enemy. The enemy is on a united front to divide the body of Christ. Since the beginning, the enemy has used a divide and conquer strategy to get us fighting the wrong battles against the wrong people.

If we see that the kingdom of darkness is united, how much more should the kingdom of God be!?

> *"Jesus knew their thoughts and said to them, "Every kingdom divided against itself will be ruined, and every city or household divided against itself will not stand. If Satan drives out Satan, he is divided against himself. How then can his kingdom stand?"*
>   - Matthew 12:25-26

What does the enemy use to divide us?

Offenses. We all have been offended by someone or a certain situation. This means being wronged, hurt, talked about in a negative way, or someone hurting someone we love. If we focus on the offense and allow it to penetrate our hearts, the results could be deadly to unity. At times, offenses can rob us of our vision and our spiritual victory. Offenses can destroy relationships. When they happen, we are left with the choice to seek reconciliation or to let go of the relationship.

Misunderstanding. This takes place when people take our words or actions out of context. Sometimes we can get offended by something that isn't even true. I remember years ago; my wife was approached by a woman before partaking in communion. The woman told my wife that she forgave her for what she had done. My wife was taken back, because she was unaware of what she had done. Many times when there is a misunderstanding some are uninformed that one took place.

People. The Bible says that we are to watch out for those who cause division. In Romans 16:17 Paul writes, "I urge you, brothers and sisters, to watch out for those who cause divisions and put obstacles in your way that are contrary to the teaching you have learned. Keep away from them." What these people do and say, is simply talk negatively about others. They may be in a place of hurt, causing them to filter all events and people from that place. The best thing to do when you're working with a person who causes division is pray for them, and if we are given an opportunity to speak into their lives, point them back to importance of fellowship and community.

Favored Mindset:
God's Favor Flows When We are United

The Bible lays upon us the responsibility of unity. This responsibility is for all of us. There isn't any of us exempt from this commandment. That begs the question; what are the duties that cultivate a habitation of unity? Paul writes about them in, Romans 12:16-18,

> *Live in harmony with one another. Do not be proud but be willing to associate with people of low position. Do not be conceited. Do not repay anyone evil for evil. Be careful to do what is right in the eyes of everyone. If it is possible, as far as it depends on you, live at peace with everyone. Do not take revenge, my dear friends, but leave room for God's wrath, for it is written: "it is mine to avenge' I will repay," says the Lord.*

At the forefront, Paul admonishes us to "live in harmony." Harmony in a music group is only possible by the band being united in rhythm and key. When harmony is achieved a melody is played. Transposing this idea to a worship team, if you have a bass player and drummer going at two different tempos and worship leader singing a song that is different than the one being played and the guitar player is missing, and the keyboardist is playing Mozart, it would be chaos. This wouldn't be a worship song ushering in the Presence of God.

Tell yourself, I have a responsibility to create a culture of unity. Every one of us has a responsibility to promote a culture of agreement. Every one of us has a responsibility to build the kingdom of God. We can't do this alone; we need each other. There isn't a lone star believer. Going to the mountains and living only with Jesus is a beautiful idea, but it isn't what He created us to do. He created us for community. There are gifts that you carry, that I don't, and visa-versa. So the millionaire dollar question is: how do we create this culture of agreement? The answer is found in our responsibility which is to be humble, to let go, to do what is right in everyone eyes and to live at peace with one another.

The Keys to Unity

Have a humble heart. Pride is something that we will all face. As we previously discovered in chapter six, spiritual pride is even harder to deal with because it makes us think that we are the only ones truly known by God. It makes us believe we are the only ones that hear from God, and the only ones with the discernment to understand the deep enigmas of the Spirit. Looking to scripture, Hebrews 3:13 says, "But encourage one another daily, as long as it is called "Today," so that none of you may be hardened by sin's deceitfulness." This verse points us in a collaborative effort to encourage each other. There isn't one who is always assigned to do the encouraging. There will be times when we will need encouragement as well.

Let it go. When we are hurt, offended and disrespected, let it go and forgive others. It isn't worth carrying. In our lives we face things that are tough, unfair, and disrespectful. The best thing to do is not harbor bitterness or resentment towards anyone.

Do what is right. There are going to be times when we want to do what's right in our own eyes. But in those moments, we need to do what is right in God's eyes. Seek reconciliation and do all you can to restore the relationship. If the party is willing to reconcile, that is a win for everyone! The kingdom has won. This is an amazing miracle that God can do in broken relationships. If you attempt to reconcile and they don't respond to your appeal, leave that at the feet of Jesus. God sees that you sought to be reconciled. You did the right thing. Now just trust the Lord to work. Your miracle may come at a time that you least expect.

Be a Peacemaker. Jesus said in the greatest sermon ever spoken, "Blessed are the peacemakers, for they will be called children of God" (Matthew 5:9). Being a peacemaker means instead of starting fires, we are putting them out. This is achievable by treating others like they're more important than yourself and recognizing that God speaks to others not only you. And respecting the decisions of others without harboring resentment towards them. Then we can focus on points that we agree on. We can all agree, Jesus is our King! We can all agree that that we need to share the Gospel to the ends of the earth. We can all agree that He's coming soon! We can all agree that we are to lift up His name. We can all agree the Word of God is true. We can all agree that the devil is a liar. What we need to do is do our part to stay one, to live in harmony, to live united, and to live in peace.

The Results

The benefits of unity are worth the effort and sacrifices to maintain it. Two things we must all recognize is our limitations and our giftings. When we acknowledge our need for community and accept help from others, the sky is the limit because we will be more effective. The power of unity is immeasurable. We will be flowing in God's anointing. The precious flow of the Holy Spirit is the most beautiful thing we can have as part of our lives. The Bible records the beauty of unity in Psalm 133, "How good and pleasant it is when brothers live together in unity! It is like precious oil poured on the head, running down on the beard, running down on Aaron's beard, down upon the collar of his robes. It is as if the dew of Hermon were falling on Mount Zion. For there the LORD bestows his blessing, even life forevermore."

The psalmist declares that is where the blessing of life forevermore is, in unity! The imagery painted here is unique. Unity is likened to anointing oil running from the top of his beautiful priestly garments. This was a special concoction and was only to be used by the priest. I can see Aaron dripping with the anointing oil running from the top his head, down his beard, then flowing on his garments. Aaron was dripping with favor! The same goes for us. When we are walking together in unity, we are dripping with favor. There is something beautiful about when we unite with each other. The anointing flows from this place of unity.

It can be equated as if the dew on Mount Hermon were to also fall on Mount Zion. We know that dew nourishes the ground, keeping things green and vibrant. Just as unity nurtures the church, keeping it alive. Mount Hermon is a snow-capped range and is the highest area in this region. These two areas are almost one hundred miles away from each other. Them being combined was impossible, but if the dew of Hermon had come together with Mount Zion, it would have been a match made in heaven. When we are walking together in unity, we too are heaven on earth.

In unity we find our destiny. These blessings are seen in the first century church. Looking again at the book of Acts, it says,

> *Now the entire group of those who believed were of one heart and mind, and no one claimed that any of his possessions was his own, but instead they held everything in common. With great power the apostles were giving testimony to the resurrection of the Lord Jesus and great grace was on all of*

them. For there not a needy person among them because all those who owned lands or houses sold them, brought the proceeds of what was sold, and laid them at the apostles' feet. This was then distributed to each person as any had need.

- Acts 4:32-35

I love that the entire church was of one heart and willing to give everything up to each other. The result was great power, the power of the Holy Spirit working in wonders and miracles. When there is unity in the body of Christ, there are miracles in our midst!

Another component that accompanied them was great grace. They boldly proclaimed the resurrection of Christ to their generation and future generations to come. This happened because of the great grace that rested upon their lives. When you have done ministry for any length of time, you know that it can be spiritually and physically depleting. The work of God is taxing work that isn't something we can sustain on our own strength. Only by God's great grace can we victoriously fulfill our mandate. The Great Commission is accomplished as a team. There is no "I" in Team Jesus.

I don't know about you, but I want to be flowing in God's anointing. I want to be united with others following the Lord. As my brother-in-law, Armando, aptly told me, "what are the first three letter in unity? U, N, I, and truly unity is only possible with You and I."

Prayer for Unity

Lord, I give you everything that can be used to divide me from others. Father remove every obstacle and wall of hindrance. Remove every scheme that divides us from each other: competition, insecurity, racism, and pride. I stand in faith against the spirit of retaliation and humbly ask for reconciliation. Let churches unite, let families unite, let generations unite, let different nationalities unite, and let marriages reunite. Let us be as one following You in faith and unity, united in holiness and grace. Let us walk in the beauty of unity. All this we ask in the Mighty Name of Jesus, Amen.

Resting in His Favor

May the favor of the Lord our God rest on us; establish the work of our hands for us— yes, establish the work of our hands.

- Psalms 90:17

"Through the dark and stormy night Faith beholds a feeble light Up the blackness streaking; Knowing God's own time is best, in a patient hope I rest for the full day-breaking!"

-John Greenleaf Whittier

At our first leaders' luncheon, we told our team of volunteers to practice a life of rest. We encouraged all of them to take a day weekly to practice the Sabbath. Some of the volunteers looked shocked, but they also appreciated our concerns for their well-being. We looked to create a culture of resting in the Lord. We are confident that our teams will be healthier, more productive, and refreshed by taking time to rest. We didn't want any one of our team members stressed out with ministry or on the verge of spiritual burnout. So, we knew that building a culture of rest was essential in accomplishing this.

Looking at Scripture, we see a rhythm of rest that God prescribed to His people. As believers we should take weekly times of rest in the Presence of God. This isn't a new idea but a pattern that God gave to us from the beginning. The Bible says in Genesis 2:2-3,

> *"And on the seventh day God ended His work which He had done, and He rested on the seventh day from all His work which He had done. Then God blessed the seventh day and sanctified it, because in it He rested from all His work which God had created and made."*

Are you tired? Drained? On the edge of a nervous breakdown? Hopefully not, but if we let the rat race of this world infect our hearts, we'll be exhausted in a race we can't win without rest. One recent article said, "Americans don't respect sleep. As much as 40 percent of us say that we don't sleep enough," it continued, "Perhaps we have too much to do or work more than one job, preventing a normal sleep routine. Whatever our reasons, sleep is often not a high priority. We shouldn't take it so lightly: there is a growing mountain of compelling evidence that our casual disregard of healthy sleep is downright dangerous."[17] The deadlines,

---

[17] https://thehill.com/opinion/healthcare/436555-americans-arent-getting-enough-sleep-and-its-killing-us?rl=1, accessed August 10, 2021.

workload, new projects, and opportunities can fill our schedules from top to bottom. Then we have our families and home responsibilities to add to the equation.

Jesus corrects us in our busyness and offers us a better way. Luke 10:38-42 says,

> *As Jesus and his disciples were on their way, he came to a village where a woman named Martha opened her home to him. She had a sister called Mary, who sat at the Lord's feet listening to what he said. But Martha was distracted by all the preparations that had to be made. She came to him and asked, "Lord, don't you care that my sister has left me to do the work by myself? Tell her to help me!" "Martha, Martha," the Lord answered, "you are worried and upset about many things, but few things are needed—or indeed only one.[a] Mary has chosen what is better, and it will not be taken away from her.*

We see from the text that Martha was busy with all the guests that were in her home. She was also distracted by all the preparations in hosting her guests. This woman was even upset with her sister for being at the feet of Jesus. Mary was in a position of rest, while Martha was in a mode of work. Jesus told her point blank, only one thing is needed, and Mary chose it. Are you a Martha; constantly busy, worried and distracted by all the preparations of life? Or are you a Mary, positioned at the feet of Jesus, receiving His strength, His wisdom, and His rest? The choice is ours.

Misguided Mindset: I Don't Have Time to Rest

Even in ministry we can work non-stop only to succumb to frustration. Are you laboring and laboring every day to see your dreams in life, ministry, or a relationship come true? No matter how hard we work or how many days we labor, only God can establish the work of our hands and hearts. Throughout my years in ministry, there have been years where I worked and worked to build God's kingdom only to see myself exhausted and drained. Being busy in ministry doesn't mean that you are living a life that is pleasing to the Lord. Busyness doesn't always equal progress. There is the workaholic mindset that doesn't take time to rest. Working in ministry could become an idol that we worship. Sacrificing a Sabbath's day of rest at the altar of work is idolatry in every sense of the word.

Sometimes there are some who cast shade at the notion of rest, thinking any sort of rest is considered laziness. However, there are distinct differences between rest and laziness. Laziness can be easily detected. It never wants to work, it's wastes time on trivial pursuits, and has no drive. Laziness doesn't want to move, sweat, or contribute. It wants to oversleep every day.

The Bible says this about laziness:

> *"Diligent hands will rule, but laziness ends in forced labor."*
>> *- Proverbs 12:24*

> *"Laziness brings on deep sleep, and the shiftless go hungry."*
>> *- Proverbs 19:15*

> *"Sluggards do not plow in season; so at harvest time they look but find nothing."*
>> *- Proverbs 20:4*

> *"A sluggard buries his hand in the dish; he is too lazy to bring it back to his mouth."*
>> *- Proverbs 26:15*

The enemy of souls is a cruel taskmaster that is bent on destroying us with one extreme or another: being lazy or a workaholic. The enemy will try to use both vices. Both are deadly, both are counterproductive, and both waste what is valuable.

Favored Mindset:
I Can Rest in God's Favor

God's example to us is one of rest. Rest is a fantastic reward after working hard. Rest should be intentional and should intertwined to our life rhythm. For this reason, God set an example for us to follow. In Deuteronomy 5:12-15 the Torah says:

> Be careful to remember the Sabbath day, to keep it holy as the LORD your God has commanded you. You are to labor six days and do all your work, but the seventh day is a Sabbath to the LORD your God. Do not do any work-you, your son or daughter, your male or female slave, your ox or donkey any of your livestock, or the resident alien who lives within your city gates, so that your male and female slaves may rest as you do. Remember that you were a slave in the land of Egypt, and the LORD your God brought you out of there with a strong hand and an outstretched arm. That is why the LORD your God has commanded you to keep the Sabbath day.

God was huge on His children getting rest. He even placed the Sabbath in the Decalogue for us to remember. This was a whole day spent resting, reflecting on God's Word and what He had done for the people of God. He said to us, "remember to rest." He gave us six days to take care of all that we are responsible for, but the seventh day was a day of rest, remembrance, and recharging. This rest was for everyone, including the servants, both female and male. God even delineated a time of rest for the animals! It was for everyone to enjoy.

God brought the people to a place of remembrance, remembering that they too were once slaves in the land of Egypt. At this moment in Israel's history, they were under cruel bondage, and assigned a heavy burden of being brick makers for the Egyptians. They worked long hours and every single day of the week. There was no weekend rest. No Labor Day vacation or holiday three-day weekends. They worked non-stop seven days a week. The Bibles says this in Exodus 2:23-24, "During that long period, the king of Egypt died. The Israelites groaned in their slavery and cried out, and their cry for help because of their slavery went up to God. God heard their groaning, and he remembered his covenant with Abraham, with Isaac and with Jacob."

As the children of Israel cried out to God, He heard their cry and came to their aid, bringing them deliverance from their bondage, and creating a new culture unlike any other nation. One of the marks that set Israel apart from every other nation was the Sabbath. The Sabbath was counter-cultural, a stark contrast to the surrounding inhabitants.

What the Sabbath Facilitates

The first thing we see is that a Sabbath reminds the people to rest in the promises of God. Knowing your entire community wasn't going to be doing work on the Sabbath had to be a huge motivating factor to not do any labor of any kind. Another motivating factor is that if they didn't, they would be stoned for breaking the Sabbath (Numbers 15:32-36).

Some may wonder why God was so strict on His people to keep the Sabbath during this time. We must remember that this man was already warned of the gravity of breaking this command. He fully knew the consequences, and if it wasn't punished, many would have been following his example of disobedience on the following Sabbath (Deuteronomy 17:7).

Although, we wouldn't physically die if we break the Sabbath these days, we die spiritually. A lack of meditating on the promises of God is a life of spiritual decline. When we miss that time to disconnect from the grid and focus on Him, we die. Let me give you an example, your cell phone when it's plugged into the charger, its battery life is fully charged after ample time of being plugged into a source of energy. If the battery life is low and you continue to use it without recharging, eventually the phone is going to die. If we apply this simple concept to our lives, we learn to practice the Sabbath and unplug from the world and connect to

God, His Word, and talking about past miracles that He has done. This is resting in His promises. In this place we are spiritually recharged.

Delighting ourselves in the Sabbath shows our dependence on Him for our sustenance, and our obedience to His commands. The book of Isaiah 58:12-14 shows us the benefits of delighting ourselves in Him when it says,

> Your people will rebuild the ancient ruins and will raise up the age-old foundations; you will be called Repairer of Broken Walls, Restorer of Streets with Dwellings. If you keep your feet from breaking the Sabbath and from doing as you please on my holy day, if you call the Sabbath a delight and the Lord's holy day honorable, and if you honor it by not going your own way and not doing as you please or speaking idle words, then you will find your joy in the Lord, and I will cause you to ride in triumph on the heights of the land.

In this powerful text, we see that when we rest in the Lord, we find supernatural joy in delighting ourselves in Him. Have you ever been lacking God's joy? This happens to us when we get distracted from the Presence of God. When we aren't living with God's Joy, we have no strength, and this is because the Joy of the Lord is our strength (Nehemiah 8:10).

Another benefit of resting in God is that we live a life of victory. The Bible promises that God will "cause you to ride in triumph on the heights of the land" (Isaiah 58: 14). We see so many people living in discouragement and despair. This promise is a powerful reminder that when we honor God, He causes us to triumph.

People have abandoned their family, spouse, friends, and church so they could work. And for what purpose? Money? Position? Prestige? The more I live, the more I realize that time is more valuable than money, because money cannot buy back time. Time is also more valuable than any position because position could make someone miserable and unable to enjoy their time. Time is also more valuable than prestige because what's the use of being prestigious if no one wants to spend time with you? Once time is gone, it's gone. When we feel like we don't have enough time to practice the Sabbath, just think, if God could rest, so could you! Believe me, God has a lot more things to do than us, and of greater importance than us, so we are without excuse.

Prayer of Rest

God, thank You for giving me an example of rest. Right now, I give You my worries, my weights, and my schedule. Let my life of rest honor You and be done in a way that is pleasing to You. From this time forward, have Your way in my calendar. Let me follow Your example of rest. Every week, let me lay aside a day where I rest, relax, and remember what You have done, and mediate on Your Word. We ask this in the Mighty Name of Jesus, Amen.

Favored by Thanksgiving

What would you think if I told you that there are no small things in life? No coincidences no matter how insignificant they may seem are lacking purpose or meaning. Every day, we get up, we go to our jobs, schools, and churches and engage in the beautiful gift of life. While on this journey of life, we can become disenchanted and lose the zeal for living. One of the ways to get there is by walking the road of "ingratitude."

This is what I would like to call a spiritual disease that affects the hearts of millions of people from every walk of life and every continent. In our generation, Americans have not faced the intense poverty levels such as the lack of drinking water, lack of adequate education, or other social ills that others have faced in third world countries. We are living in a free country with laws set up in our favor. We are allowed the opportunity to create, distribute, and profit. This fuels dreamers. Not all countries allow their citizens to do that. They decide what you do and where you do it. Now, as Americans, we are privileged because brave women and men have literally given their lives so we may have those freedoms.

If we have this freedom in our county why does it seem that there is a great distain for America among its own young people? Why are so many ungrateful? The pictures we see today on the news are heartbreaking: vandalism of innocent businesses, lawlessness, burning of the Bible, resistant to authority, and a hatred towards God. As a country founded on Judeo-Christian values, how could we drift so far?

The Bible gives us the answer to this in Paul's letter to his apprentice Timothy which says, "For men will be lovers of themselves, lovers of money, boasters, proud, blasphemers, disobedient to parents, unthankful, unholy" (2 Timothy 3:2). The context of this verse reveals how the people in the end times will be living. Any student of biblical eschatology easily sees our world today living in those times. I would agree that the time is near. If the proverbial clock is ticking many of us would say that it's at 11:59. But regardless of when Christ is going to return, we all know that we need to live with a mindset of certainty in our convictions and not become lazy or unthankful in our walk with the Lord. This is especially true in the area of thanksgiving. As believers that is one of our greatest privileges to live a life of thanksgiving to our Lord. Not only a privilege, but also a command found all throughout Scripture, over and over again.

For example, 1 Thessalonians 5:18 says,

"Give thanks in all circumstances for this is God's will for you in Christ Jesus." And in Psalms 100:4, the Word says, "Enter His gates with thanksgiving and His courts with praise; give thanks to Him and praise His name." Finally, Ezra 3:11 says, "With praise and thanksgiving they sang to the Lord."

Now one of the most profound stories of thanksgiving can be found starting in Luke 17:11. Let's take a look:

Now it happened as He went to Jerusalem that He passed through the midst of Samaria and Galilee. Then as He entered a certain village, there met Him ten men who were lepers, who stood afar off. And they lifted up their voices and said, "Jesus, Master, have mercy on us!"

So when He saw them, He said to them, "Go, show yourselves to the priests." And so it was that as they went, they were cleansed. And one of them, when he saw that he was healed, returned, and with a loud voice glorified God, and fell down on his face at His feet, giving Him thanks. And he was a Samaritan. So Jesus answered and said, "Were there not ten cleansed? But where are the nine? Were there not any found who returned to give glory to God except this foreigner?" And He said to him, "Arise, go your way. Your faith has made you well.

- Luke 17:11-19

The life of a leper in Jesus' day was a sad situation. Without modern medicine and clinical advances, lepers were in a hopeless state. These men and women were outcasted and not allowed to associate with others. They lived lonely lives far off from the community. If anyone came too close to them, the leper was to shout aloud that he was unclean to protect the community. The leper's quality of life was this:

- They had an incurable condition
- They didn't have non-leper friends
- They were unworthy to associate with friends and family
- They were not allowed to enter the temple to worship God
- They were totally isolated from others

So when the one healed leper, the Sarmatian, came back to Jesus to honor Him for the miracle of being made whole, this was a profound measure of thankfulness. Because the return ratio was marginal. Out of 10 men, 10 men who were outcasts because of their condition, only 1 came back. This was a total disgrace to grace.

Misguided Mindset:
I Don't Have Anything to be Thankful For

Sadly, these men made a grave mistake in not coming back. Jesus took note and even mentioned that nine were missing. We see here that it's easy not to go back. We seem to be hardwired to overlook gratitude. In the hustle and bustle of life, we get too busy to reflect, and humbly go back to the feet of Jesus and give Him the glory for what He has done in our lives.

We must always remember that we too were helpless lepers, diseased by spiritual leprosy. Without God sin ruled our lives, and we had an incurable condition. We didn't get the profound privilege of entering the Presence of God. We were cut off from God. Until one day, Jesus came down a road at an intersection in our lives. Dear Jesus met us in our worst moment. I personally still remember that moment. It brings me to tears to know that the Creator of the heavens and earth could love a man like me. And not only love me, but also love you. Right now, reflect on that time when He forgave you of your sins.

Favored Mindset:
I'm Thankful for All God Has Done,
Is Doing, and Will Do in My Life

What is God doing in your life in this season? If look carefully we will discover that He is doing so much.

But there are also things that God is doing that will be undetected because He is working in our blind spots. These occurrences are like when you lose your keys and it causes you to avoid an accident, or when you're late for work but were spared from some unforeseen misfortune. This is one of the great mysteries of the Christian walk: God in His Providence being our "rearguard." Then there are more obvious instances of protection, provision, and direction He paints on the canvas of our lives. Instances where we recognize what we have been spared from. What God has spared us from is something that requires us to look at our lives, and ask, "Where would I be right now if I never accepted Jesus into my life?" What was the trajectory of my life with the decisions I was making? What direction was I headed in? When we consider these factors honestly, we discover what you and I have been spared from.

This type of reflection should also cause us to recognize and be sensitive to what others are facing. Even today, there are many people who have lost so much in California in the wake of the wildfires raging all throughout the state. I was watching an interview from a woman who was rummaging through her house that was caught in the blaze. She had so lost so much. From one day to the next, this woman like hundreds of others, lost all her possessions. It's heartbreaking.

Recently like so many others, I contracted Covid-19. I wasn't seeming to recover. So after 10 days at my house, I finally went to the emergency department at the local hospital. When I arrived, there were so many people in terrible pain. I saw a toddler wheeled in on stretcher, and an elderly woman in so much pain because something was stuck in her throat, and then a young man with an amputee leg, in pain because his leg was deeply infected. As I looked at their faces, it was a reminder that we all face suffering, even if you're a Christian. No one is exempt. Because my oxygen levels were dangerously low, I was admitted to a room. As I was being admitted, I thought, "Wow, I have to face this, and God is using a different road to my recovery than I thought fit." But regardless He is God, and I'm glad He did it that way. It brought a new level of sensitivity in my heart towards others who are in tough circumstances. I appreciate that He allowed that to take place.

Gratitude is the master key to recognizing the blessings of God in our lives. For any building, there is a master key that gives access to all the rooms of that building. No other key could open all those doors the way the master key can open them. Only that copy of the master key has the power to open everything. In our Christian walk, there is a master key to all the blessings of God in our lives, and it is the master key of thanksgiving. Here are a couple of reasons to be thankful today: God's Love. Psalm 107:43 says,

> *"Whoever is wise, let him attend to these things; let them consider the steadfast love of the LORD."*

The love of God is beyond anything we can describe or imagine. When I think about Him loving me while I was still dead in my sins and trespasses, I am astounded. The idea that a Holy God could love an unholy sinner always confounds me, and that in His mercy, He sought me and bought me by His precious ransom on the Cross. The Cross is the greatest picture of love in action. It embodies the message of the Gospel. A loving King coming to die in place of his dying subjects. His love is the game-changer for all humanity. A Love to be thankful for. God will always help His faithful ones. Be thankful for His help. Isaiah 41:10 says,

> *"fear not, for I am with you; be not dismayed, for I am your God; I will strengthen you, I will help you, I will uphold you with my righteous right hand."*

Thank God for His help! He never abandons us or leaves us by ourselves. The Bible constantly reminds us that He won't forsake us. This is an encouraging promise. When the Lord started Remnant, we sometimes worried where the resources would come from. Thankfully, God always provided, He always helped. He is a Good Father! This verse came alive in our lives as a church so powerfully, Philippians 4:19,

> *"And my God will supply every need of yours according to his riches in glory in Christ Jesus."*

Thanksgiving opens the door to His Presence

There is no other way to enter into the Presence of God other than by praise and thanksgiving. When You and I begin to give God thanks for what He has done, it opens the door to the Presence of God. When we are thankful, it knocks down walls of the enemy. There is a shift in the atmosphere. The spiritual forces can hear the song of our hearts and it affects the heavens. Truly, every trial we face can be won with thanksgiving and songs of praise. As we sing and make a song in our hearts, our breakthrough comes! Let's always remember what Christ has healed us from in our lives. He notices our gratitude. And because we are so favored, we should always be singing songs of thanksgiving to our King. Let's not let ingratitude rob us any longer of the great gift of thanksgiving to our God. He deserves it, and His favor rests on those possess it.

Prayer of Thanksgiving

Dear Heavenly Father, thank You for leading me in my life by your precious Holy Spirit. My journey has been marked by ups and downs, but in every situation I'm thankful that you have seen me through. You have been faithful each step of the way. In my busyness, I know that I have missed opportunities to thank You. Lord, please forgive me. I'm sorry and I repent from my lack of thanksgiving. Thank You Lord for all You have done in my life. From this day forward, I will live a life of thanksgiving, In Jesus Mighty Name, Amen.

Favored for Success

"Keep this book of the Law always on your lips; mediate on it day and night, so that you may be careful to do everything written in it. Then you will be prosperous and successful. Have I not commanded you? Be strong and courageous. Do not be afraid: do not be discouraged, for the Lord your God will be with you wherever you go."

- Joshua 1:8-9

"The foundation stones for a balanced success are honesty, character, integrity, faith, love and loyalty."

- Zig Ziglar

When we were kids we all possessed sublime dreams of being successful in life. Our dreams drove us to conferences, colleges, to seek mentors and for many of us, to study like crazy! When we think about success there are so many different ideas that come to mind.

We can define it by things that are measurable such as budgets, financial portfolios, and overall growth. Other ways we can find ourselves defining success is by having outward possessions, cars, and houses. Then there are successes we may define on a relational spectrum such as having good, lasting friendships or magnanimous marriages.

The Hebrew word for success is the word "sakal," which means: to be prudent, act wisely, comprehend, discern, to have insight; while God's Word defines it as an inward quality that affects how we conduct ourselves in this world. God's Word gives us context that guides us on how to honor God and His creation. True success is having God's wisdom in our lives. This leads us to make Godly decisions that honor God and others. While on the other hand, living a life according to our flesh will hinder us from living a prosperous and successful life which God intended.

After a midweek service recently, I went out to eat with one of our pastors. As we were eating, an older gentleman came up to us and told us that God loved us, and we mentioned that we were believers. He excitedly called his friend over to meet us. His friend was retiring from pastoring at the age of 74, as he had been a faithful shepherd for many decades. I noticed from the moment I met him; he had a very humble spirit. He was a Vietnam veteran, and he lead a Christian support group for veterans. To be in the presence of a man who had made it to this point in his life, I knew I had to ask him what the secret to a long, faithful ministry was. So I did. He said these words with great confidence, "Keep your eyes on Jesus and watch out for the enemy's schemes." These golden words of wisdom are profound, simple, and true.

Misguided Mindset:
I can be Successful Without God in My Life

After this encounter, the Pastor I was eating with recalled 2 Corinthians 2:11, where Paul writes, "In order that Satan might not outwit us. For we are not unaware of his schemes." The term outwit means to take advantage of, to trick, to fool. There are so many traps set up by the enemy that want to destroy our lives. Three ways the enemy of our souls works to trap and outwit us are these:

We forget about God after He gives us success. If we are honest, this is so easy to do. God brings success and then we forget about Him. In life, there will be people who come alongside us and teach us certain principles that will empower us. What could even happen is you take those principles or tricks they taught and refine them, making them even more effective. When this happens, a dilemma could occur. We can begin to forget that we wouldn't know these things or have this knowledge in the first place if it weren't for our mentors. They were sent by God to teach us and someday we will teach others. Sadly, we could forget about our mentors and in effect, we are forgetting about God.

We forget to give God the glory. This one is extremely, extremely dangerous. There is a realm that only God walks in, and His Name is to be deeply reverenced. God is so "Other," and beyond human comprehension or anything we imagine. For example, even our idle words that we speak haphazardly, we will give an account for those to God (Matthew 12:36-37). If that seems foreign to us, that's because God is beyond us. With Him being in that place, we have been endowed with the great privilege to give Him glory. When we give Him glory, His glory shines down upon us. This is a great privilege but also a dangerous place because if we are not giving that glory back to Him, He could remove us from the privilege of ministry instantly. Let me provide an example. Years ago I pastored a church in the small town of Porterville, and we wanted to rent a small church building. So I began to call different churches, and this church in particular sent me to voicemail and the voicemail from their pastor stated, "We are the most anointed church in town." After hearing the message, I was blown away by their self-confidence. Although they were successful, I felt it was unhealthy to broadcast it. Sadly, a few years later the church was hit so hard when the Pastor had a moral failure. The church was crushed.

We forget that God could remove success from us at any moment. At any moment God could put the brakes on us. Success is a comfortable place when the hand of the Lord is upon us. We almost seem invincible because of the anointing that rests upon us: people are following us, ministry is growing, and the results are evident. In those moments we can never trust in our own abilities but trust the One who gave us the ability. The anointing of God doesn't mean we can live unaccountable lives, and it doesn't mean we are 100% correct in everything. When God elevates us with success, we must strive to stay on our knees in total humility of our abilities.

Favored Mindset:
I'm Going to be Successful
in All that I Put My Heart To

Now looking at the favored mindset in the context of success, I believe God wants us to live successful lives. This encompasses the Hebrew word sakal, which again means to live prudently. The keys that I have been taught by my parents, teachers, pastors, mentors and life experience have given me a glimpse of what sakal means in real life and how to possess it. These are the keys for obtaining sakal.

Stay in God's Word every day. We recently challenged some our church to read 7 chapters of the Bible every day. It has been quite the experience. It has taught us discipline and has put us on the fast track to read the whole Bible twice a year! But more importantly, it's obedience to God's Word. The Bible says in 1 Peter

2:2-3, "Like newborn babies, crave pure spiritual milk, so that by it you may grow up in your salvation, now that you have tasted that the Lord is good." The Word of God gives us wisdom. It leads us to make the right decisions. It strengthens our convictions. When we immerse ourselves in God's Word, the Holy Spirit is working within our lives. Our lives become recalibrated. With the constant onslaught we face from the enemy, we need to constantly be hearing back the Word of God. As we abide in His Word, life and spiritual nourishment are flooded back in our lives! Just like we need to eat every day, we need to read God's Word every day to nourish our spirit.

Choose your friends wisely. One of the most powerful verses in the Bible dealing with choosing your friends is Proverbs 13:20, which says, "Walk with the wise and become wise, for a companion of fools suffers harm." We like to believe that we are free thinkers who are only influenced by ourselves, but that idea is not true. We are impacted most by those whom we spend most of our time with. Journalist, Malcolm Gladwell, wrote, "We like to think of ourselves as inner-directed, that who we are and how we act is something permanently set by our genes and our temperament. We are actually powerfully influenced by our surroundings, our immediate context, and the personalities of those around us." What Mr. Gladwell wrote reinforces the idea of choosing your friends wisely. Our friends set us on a trajectory towards a destination. Let us be with the right friends on the right trajectory.

Value others. We have all been graced by God with beautiful people in our lives. Our parents, siblings, coworkers, friends, and spouses are gifts from God to us. We can never look at people like we are better than them or think that, because we aren't better than anyone. Scripture clearly reveals that even us leaders must be examples to the flock. 1 Peter 5:3 says, "not Lording it over those entrusted to you, but being examples to the flock." Peter was effectively saying leaders should treat the people entrusted to their care with respect and dignity. Transposing this to our lives as leaders--we need to treat others with respect and not talk down to people, belittle, slander or gossip about them. People are precious. Even the ones that give us problems. We are all in need of grace. Not one of us is perfect. Only Jesus! So how can we value others? First, apologize when you fail. Taking responsibility for our shortcomings is huge. It shows character and character counts. It's the currency that people are willing to follow. Secondly, forgiveness is something we do daily. I know we covered a whole chapter on the topic of forgiveness. That's definitely a chapter for constant review. When we value others, we are willing to forgive them. They may offend us and instead of harboring a grudge, we are to forgive them and value them. As Christians, we should never give up on people.

Watch for pinch points. A pinch point is an area in between moving and stationary parts of a machine where an individual's body part may become caught, leading to injury or even death. In life, there are pinch points that we want to avoid. There are going to times when people are going to encourage you to go to places without telling you the consequences of them. These places land us in compromising situations that could lead us down a dark road. These pinch points don't look dangerous, but they are. Something to consider, one safeguard that was taught to me was never to be alone with a female during counseling sessions. Because of this wise counsel that was instructed to me, I have always had my wife with me when conducting counseling sessions. This has worked as a safeguard against many devices of the enemy.

Keep our eyes focused on Jesus. Just like the retiring Pastor, in the story I mentioned earlier, told me, keep your eyes focused on Jesus—it is what keeps us. It's not the pats on back, it's not the full crowds, and it's not the speaking engagements that keep us. What keeps us is having our hearts focused on Jesus. You see, disappointment will come, sickness strikes, jobs can be lost, but where do we turn in those moments? We turn to Jesus. When we have our eyes focused on Jesus, He leads us with His peace and His strength. We are supplied with the comfort that is needed. We find God's perfect sakal in our lives. Our greatest privilege in life is to know God, to focus solely on Him, and to have a relationship with Him. That is the true definition of success.

Prayer of Success

Father thank You for the privilege You have entrusted me with. All I do is for Your glory. I'm humbled by that privilege. Lord enable me to have a clean heart as success comes into my life. Let me harness it in a way that honors You. Let me always remember I'm simply a messenger but not the One who wrote the message. As I go forward, let Your success flood my life, let it touch others for Your glory. Give me Your "sakal" in my heart, always knowing that everything comes from Your hands and is entrusted in my hands for only the times and seasons that You see fit. All this I pray in the Mighty Name of Jesus, Amen.

About the Author

Danny along with his lovely wife Sabrina serve as the lead Pastors of the Remnant church in Whittier, California. Danny and Sabrina have been married for over nineteen years and have four beautiful teenage children, Danny Jr., Zeriah, Noah, and Nehemiah. Sabrina and Danny desire to glorify God and lead a new generation to do the same (1 Timothy 4:12). Danny is the author of Through the Eyes of a Prodigal. His preaching style is described as transparent, encouraging, and practical. Danny is a graduate of Vision International University, with a bachelor's degree in Ministry, and is currently working on his master's degree from Vision International University. Danny and Sabrina reside with their family and two small dogs Titus and Abbey in Los Angeles county. Learn more at *DannyCasasJr.com*